MYSTERIES VEDIC FACE READING

HRISHIKESH DUBEY

JAICO PUBLISHING HOUSE

Ahmedabad Bangalore Bhopal Bhubaneswar Chennai
Delhi Hyderabad Kolkata Lucknow Mumbai

Published by Jaico Publishing House
A-2 Jash Chambers, 7-A Sir Phirozshah Mehta Road
Fort, Mumbai - 400 001
jaicopub@jaicobooks.com
www.jaicobooks.com

MYSTERIES OF VEDIC FACE READING
ISBN 978-81-8495-130-1

First Jaico Impression: 2011
Fifth Jaico Impression: 2016

Illustrations by Mayur Mistry

Printed by
Repro India Limited
Plot No. 50/2, T.T.C. MIDC Industrial Area
Mahape, Navi Mumbai - 400 710

This book is entirely dedicated to
The Lotus Feet of My Lord
The Supreme Personality of Godhead
Sri Krishna

Everybody is born ordinary with the right to become extraordinary and great minds have purposes, whereas others simply have wishes.

—Hrishikesh Dubey

CONTENTS

PART II – INDIVIDUAL FACIAL FEATURES

AUTHOR'S NOTE

............MUST READ

No work in this universe is completely the work of a single person. There are many unnamed people behind the scenes and mystical divine powers behind certain people or work. This work of divine origin is a masterpiece in itself as the prompter of Vedic face reading and body reading is the Supreme Personality of Godhead Sri Krishna Himself. The knowledge given in this book is passed on through a *parampara* system in a disciplic succession, in accordance with the injunctions of the scriptures, so it is a highly confidential and authoritative knowledge which is revealed in the most accurate and bona fide form for the benefit of the mankind.

This book has been rightly named *Mysteries of Vedic Face Reading* as till date this knowledge remains a mystery for the common masses and only certain people who have access to the Vedic wisdom in the *parampara* system have this knowledge and access to other mystical and esoteric teachings of the Vedas. Such highly authoritative, confidential and esoteric knowledge was never imparted to the people outside the disciplic succession as a proper spiritual training is required before a person becomes eligible for such knowledge. Vedas stress a lot upon the purity of mind, body, and spirit before the beginning and initiation of spiritual knowledge. Only those people who will assimilate the author's note and strictly adhere and abide by the instructions given herein will thoroughly benefit from this book and will definitely become successful in all their endeavours and soon discover new dimensions in life.

The speaker of this knowledge is Lord Sri Krishna Himself, so anyone who wishes to accept this knowledge and relish its essence should duly consider Lord Sri Krishna as the Supreme Personality of Godhead because He is mentioned on every page of the *Bhagavad Gita* as the Supreme Personality of Godhead and is regarded as the *Para Brahma* and Supreme Personality of Godhead throughout the *Vedas*, the *Brahma Sutra* and the *Puranas*. This is a humble attempt to present this knowledge in the same *parampara* system in order to establish the Krishna consciousness movement more soundly and progressively.

As this work is of divine origin and has self-inculcated divine and mystical powers within it, and since all the people who have had and who used this knowledge were divine people, gods, or demigods so to interpret this knowledge or any part of it in any form without the will of Krishna is the greatest offence. This book has been written and brought out for the public with the will of Krishna.

So people engaged in cultivation of this knowledge should do so with faith in an honest way to get the rewards and fruits of their hard work. These people should not be envious of Krishna in any way and should have high regard for Krishna and His devotees. People engaged in the unauthorised reproduction or study of this book to fulfil any personal ambitions without giving their due to the authorised people, who have worked on this book and without any regard for the *Vaishnavas* and Krishna, would be engaging in immoral activity and burdening themselves with such an obligation whose due will remain with them throughout this life and hereafter. Such people will have no future either in this world or the next and will have no future thereafter. So this is the foremost advice to people who are engaged in reading this book, they should buy only the original copy of this book to get the real nectar of knowledge given in this book and should shun all the unauthorised publications of this book completely.

Being a transcendentalist in disciplic succession of Sri Krishna I request every reader of this book to wholeheartedly contribute

towards promoting Krishna Consciousness to promote spiritual
development, peace and prosperity in this world and to elevate
themselves on the zenith of success on physical, mental,
emotional, financial, and spiritual levels.

Hari Bol.

INTRODUCTION

The human form that we get and the events that occur in our life, are not the product of our actions in this birth. They are the accumulated product of the actions of many births. If this wasn't the case then some people wouldn't have been rich; some wouldn't have been wise; some wouldn't have been joyful, while others wouldn't have been miserable. We all would have been equal and have had the same platform to start our life from. Our life would have started afresh, from the very first scratch. However, our life never starts from scratch; our life is the product of all our previous lives, including our thoughts, deeds, and consciousness at the time of death.

My sole purpose of writing this book is to make everyone understand what Vedic knowledge is, and to pass on this knowledge as it is, revealed to me in a bona fide disciplic succession. My purpose is to present the revelation of the Supreme Lord as it was revealed by Him, and not that of any mundane speculator who has construed his own thoughts and created an unauthorised book on face reading, body reading, or other metaphysical sciences.

According to the books written by some previous oriental and occidental physiognomists, who are not in disciplic succession and who do not have any bonafide spiritual background, oriental and occidental face-reading/astrology is based on five elements —

Wood, Metal, Water, Fire and Earth. This philosophy is absolutely untrue, the thesis of which seems to be absurd. In their philosophy of five elements, the last three elements — Water, Fire, and Earth — are correct, but the first two elements — Wood and Metal — are incorrect. However according to the *Vedas* and the *Bhagavad Gita* there are eight principal manifestations in material energy and those are Earth, Water, Fire, Air, Ether (or Sky), Mind, Intelligence, and False Ego. These eight elements constitute Krishna's material energies. Of these eight, the first five — Earth, Water, Fire, Air, and Sky — are gross material elements and the other three — mind, intelligence, and false ego — are subtle material energies. Every single person in this material world is made up of these eight material elements and there are no other material energies, or elements. The Soul is the fragmental part and parcel of the Supreme Lord, that is not at all material and is considered to be the superior energy responsible for life on any planet.

The science of Astrology takes into account the gross material elements — Earth, Water, Fire, Air, and Sky. Among these five elements, only the first four elements — Earth, Water, Fire, and Air — are considered for calculations or predictions in astrology, face reading, body reading etc. The fifth element — Sky (or Ether) — is neutral because of its neutral effect upon the human body. According to the Vedas, the fifth element plays a major role only for Heavenly planets, like Heaven, where the compositions of the bodies of living entities are different and where totally different laws of physics operate.

So, refer to any part of astrology, numerology, or any other Vedic science like face reading, or body reading and you will always find the prominence of these four elements only. There is no other element apart from these four elements that plays any role. That's the reason why the twelve months in the calendar year are also divided into the twelve signs of zodiac and all the twelve signs fall into one of these four elements only. There is no other element like Wood or Metal, because they are never counted separately. If wood disintegrates, you will find that the major portion of wood comprises the Earth element, and it contains small portions of Water, Fire, and Air within it. Again metal is extracted from the earth and is part of earth itself.

The purpose of this book is to bring out the truth about how to determine the real nature, character, personality, and the whole destiny of a person; no matter how hard a person tries to fake his true personality. Vedic physiognomy will help people determine each and every person's socio-political beliefs as well. It helps in understanding people who are honest and truthful and those who are dishonest and untruthful, because people who pretend will not be able to stop the truth from revealing itself on their face.

We hope, therefore, that this book will help people get close to reality and to ascertain the truth about each human being they associate with. Also, this book will ensure that readers will not get influenced by the so-called leaders who misguide people and play with their emotions just to fulfil their personal ambitions. This book has been designed and written in such a way that even novices who are interested in the science of face reading can easily learn and understand it, and derive numerous benefits from it. This is powerful knowledge that is revealed in a bona fide disciplic succession, and after reading this book, the lives of many won't remain the same.

PART I

Fundamentals of
Vedic Face Reading

DIVISION OF THE FACE

RIGHT   LEFT

The face is divided vertically and horizontally as illustrated in the above diagram. The details of division of the face are discussed in the following chapters.

CHAPTER 1

VERTICAL DIVISION OF THE FACE

THE LEFT AND THE RIGHT SIDES OF THE FACE: THE SHIV AND THE SHAKTI PRINCIPLES

Before starting face reading, hypothetically divide the person's face into half, the left and the right sides, by drawing an imaginary line vertically down the centre of the face from the top of the forehead to the chin. One should keep in mind that 'left' refers to the left-hand side of the person being read. So, if you are looking at somebody else's face, face to face, your right-hand side is directly opposite to the person's left-hand side and your left-hand side is directly opposite to their right. However, if you are looking at your own image in a mirror, your left is the reflection's left. Wave at yourself in the mirror with your left hand, then your right hand, and you will see what I mean.

When you draw the imaginary vertical line down the middle of any face, you will observe that the face is not exactly symmetrical. You can observe this about yourself. The right eye is different from the left eye, and the right side of the face varies in minute details at least, if compared to the left side. Try and notice all the differences between the left half and the right half of the face. Everything counts, including the differences in symmetry, lines on both sides, eyebrows, eyes, inclination of the nose, nostrils, cheeks, ears, etc. The more noticeable the difference, the more significant the meaning.

VERTICAL DIVISION OF THE FACE

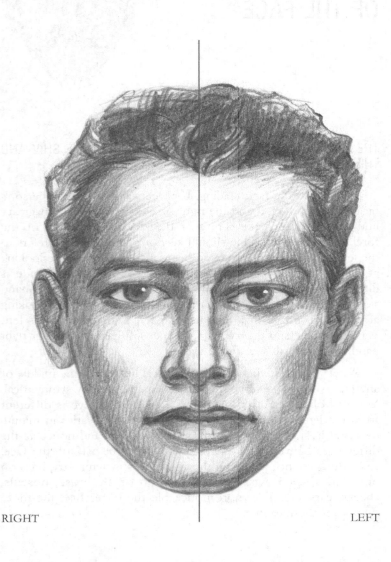

RIGHT   LEFT

It is a scientific fact that the left half of our brain controls the right side of our body including everything on the right side of our face, while the right half of our brain controls everything on the left side of our body including the left side of our face.

As the brain is divided into two hemispheres, likewise the body is also divided into two hemispheres according to Vedic science, which says that due to the law of creation, the brains, of both men and women, function differently because of the different purposes of their creation.

The vibrations in the body are based upon the two principles, i.e. Shiva and Shakti principles. The right side of the body is controlled by the Shiva principle and the left side of the body is controlled by the Shakti principle. The Shiva principle is also similar to, or comparable with the Yang principle and the Shakti principle is similar to or comparable with the Yin principle. So, the right side of the body is the male side and the left side of the body is the female side.

The Chinese and American face readers have made a gross mistake in their observation about this principle. According to them, the left side of the body is Yang (male side) and the right side of the body is Yin (female side), which is one hundred percent incorrect as per the fundamentals of Vedic face reading. I don't know how these Chinese and American face readers have developed their philosophies, the thesis of which seems to be totally incorrect. The right side of the body or the face can never be the female side logically, or scientifically. If we go as per logic, then the right side is always the dominant side of the body as most of the work is performed by the right part of the body itself, that's the reason why majority of the population throughout the world is right-handed. Take into consideration any religion, all of them agree that God has made men and women so that both could easily adjust to each other because of their innate nature. The characteristics of manhood are dominance, roughness, and impetuosity, while weakness, tenderness, and sensibility are the distinguishing features of womanhood. So, as the right side of the body is the dominant side, so the right side is always the male/yang side and never the female/yin side. This is what logic says.

Let's study what science says. Science says that men mostly process information from the left side of the brain and as the left side of the brain controls the right-hand side of the body, so the right-hand side of the body is the male side, scientifically as well. So, whether you are a right-handed person, or left-handed, the right side of the body will always remain the male/Shiva/Yang side and the left side of the body always remains the female/Shakti/Yin side.

Now, one more fact about the left and the right sides in Vedic face reading is that, the right side, apart from being the male side also represents the spiritual side, and the left side, apart from being the female side, represents the material side, for both sexes. It is due to this principle that the right side is always considered to be the Shiva side, which represents the Supreme Yogi, or a transcendentalist always in a trance and the left side is considered to be the Shakti side which is nothing but the *atma-maya* of the Lord. So the left side represents the material side or nescience and the right side of the face or the body represents the transcendental side. This fact holds true if one refers to the *Ardha-nareshwara* (half-man and half-women) deity Shiva. Again, one can also notice striking differences between the material and spiritual worshippers of Ganpati. Ganpati's trunk is always pointing to the right-hand side in the spiritual worshippers of Ganpati, while the trunk of Ganpati will point towards the left-hand side, for the material worshippers of Ganpati. This means that for material gains, people worship that deity of Ganpati whose trunk is pointing towards the left-hand side, however those seeking spiritual bliss worship Ganpati whose trunk is directed towards the right-hand side. However, it should be noted that worshipping Ganpati with the trunk directed to the right is always prefered, because this Ganpti is considered to be more auspicious than the Ganpati with the trunk on the left-hand side. This is so because people who worship Ganpati with the trunk pointing towards the right-hand side get all their material desires fulfilled as well, apart from being spiritually blessed, as Ganpati always bestows goodness to people from the right side, by moving his trunk from right to left, since His trunk is originally said to be situated on the right hand side of His body.

It is very important in face reading to know that if the subject is male and if the left-hand side of his face is more pronounced than the right-hand side then this means he will care more for women and he will be very materialistic, with little or no desire for spiritual activities. So, he will prioritise women and pleasure ahead of everything else. If this is the case, he will be very attracted towards women and will have a very strong desire to have sexual intercourse with every beautiful girl he comes across.

To get a better and clearer picture, check which side of the face the nose tilts towards. If the nose of a man tilts towards the left then he is certainly very inclined towards women and pleasure. If the nose of the man tilts towards his left, he is certainly polygamous. If such people are film producers or filmmakers, then it can be said that they will have sexual relationships with almost all the female actors they have ever worked with.

If a woman's left-hand side of the face is more pronounced than the right-hand side, or if her nose tilts to the left-hand side of her face then she will be very self-centred, as the left side of the face is their own side and the right side of the face is the male side. However, if the right-hand side of a woman's face is fuller or more pronounced than the left-hand side, or if her nose tilts to the right-hand side then this woman will have more male influences in her life and might be more giving in personal relationships. This is the behavioural part of personal relationships. Now, let's briefly learn about how men and women function differently in the business world and other spheres of life.

Vedic face reading is of the view that the dominant side is always the public side, for both men and women. For example, if a person (man or woman) is right-handed, his/her dominant side is the right side and hence the right half of the body is the public side. Similarly for left-handed people, the dominant side is the left-hand side; hence the left-hand side of the body is their public side. The various aspects of the dominant side show the public personality, and the aspects of the non-dominant side show the private personality. If one notices substantial asymmetry between the two sides of the face, then the person:

(1) Might not always obey rules

(2) Might have substantial differences between how he/she behaves with colleagues, compared to the family

(3) Might be highly adaptable and flexible, etc.

As mentioned earlier, for men, the right is their own side and represents their own personality and the right side of the face will represent the business or the public side as well (if the man is right-handed). A man whose right side of the face is more pronounced and broader will focus more on business relationships rather than his own self.

It should be very clear that the right side of the face and the body indicates the spiritual side of the person as well, so even if these people are not into business, still they will be more humble, polite, and kind to others because of their philanthropic natures. They are friendlier on a personal level and share a close personal bond with each of their friends and business colleagues and even with those who are not so well-known to them. These people are warmer with others than the vice-a-versa male category. They are people whom you can trust and confide in, as they keep secrets only to themselves.

On the other hand, the men whose left sides are more pronounced as compared to the right, or whose nose tilts towards the left side of their face, will focus more upon women in business as well. Remember, these people (men and women) are more materialistic, so the fulfilment of their own material desires is more important for them, rather than anything else.

Let's look at the women, whose left side is their own side. If she is right-handed (which majority of them are), then the right side of their face is the public side. In this case the public side becomes common for both right-handed men and women. As for men, the right side of the face is the side that represents their own personality and portrays their business side as well, men tend to be better in business dealings rather than women. This happens because they are good at understanding the other person's needs, wants, priorities, and demands because they possess the ability to see things on a personal level (since the right side is their personal, and business, as well as spiritual side). So as per the Vedic viewpoint, it is the man who should take care of the business and women should take care of the home because for women, the left is their own side, which is the Shakti/Yin side, or the material side, which is known as the more greedy and receptive side. So, women are mostly concerned with the fulfilment of their own material ambitions rather than concentrating upon business, or personal relationships. So, women tend to be innately greedier, when compared to men, by the basic nature of creation. The Vedas are of the opinion that if women tend to venture into public, then they will tend to use the Yang or the Shiva side, which is not their own side and hence it might create an imbalance in the way they function. An imbalance might happen because men are better in understanding the public at the personal level, while women tend to follow differences.

Now, let us scientifically discuss the aforementioned logical statements. As the brain is divided into two hemispheres, the left hemisphere is responsible for logic and arithmetic, while the right hemisphere is responsible for creativity and intuition. The right part of our brain also controls our emotions. The function of the left brain can be described as dividing the world into a monad of data, which we organise into a logical sequence to predict outcomes. Our left brain is like our computer. It is concerned with facts, logic, data, and linear time and this is reflected on the right side of our face. But, the right half of our brain is concerned with non-linear consciousness. Men mostly use the left side of their brain to process any information and as the left side of the brain controls the right side of the face and the body, hence the right side is always the male side, as has been explained earlier.

However for women, this is not the case. Women generally use both sides of their brain to process information, because if women use only the left half of their brains (like men) for processing information, they might not be able to receive information accurately. That's the reason why both sides of their brain function simultaneously for processing even the smallest and simplest details. For men, the functions of both the hemispheres of the brain are independent and separate and men use the right side of their brain only when they are working on intricate and complex issues, or subjects.

We can clearly distinguish the exact differences between the functions of the brains of both sexes by considering the above mentioned facts. As women mostly use both sides of the brain, they might be good at mugging information and remembering things. Since men only use the left side of their brain to process information and as the functions of the left and the right hemispheres of the brain are separate for men, they are usually good at the practical application of that knowledge and are better equipped for handling worldly affairs. We generally see women behaving in a very conservative way and acting in a stereotypical fashion unless some social or political changes are brought into effect, because they generally follow the functions of society and their emotions, while men, who are generally more interested in intricate details and in using their imagination, believe in experimenting with new things and believe in abrupt social and political changes.

As per Vedic literature, the areas in the brain that are highly advanced and evolved are the frontal part, which as the name implies is right behind the forehead and, then the back part of the brain, which is in the left side at the back. In modern science, these sections or areas are called the association cortex which means that these areas are more highly advanced, more highly evolved then the other parts of the brain. Therefore, if one has to compare the differences between a genius' brain with that of a normal person, then one would look at these regions. If one closely observes a genius' brain then one would be astonished to find that the ratio of cells in these regions differ when compared to a normal person. For example, Einstein's brain had more Glial cells per neuron (per nerve cell), than the average man. Again the probability of a genius's brain being larger and heavier than the normal person is high. Lenin's brain was larger and heavier than that of the average man.

The Vedas also state that in the ages before this Age of Kali, people possessed brains that were many times heavier and larger as compared to people in this Age. That's the reason our forefathers were able to unlock the secrets of the universe even while sitting in some remote place on earth. It is so amazing that although no rockets or satellites were sent into space in the ancient times, yet the Vedas contain intricate descriptions about how the universe was formed and how the universe functions. Everything, right from the description of the nine planets in the solar system, to the big bang theory, atoms, molecules etc., and several other topics, have been discussed thoroughly in Vedic literature, written thousands of years ago itself. This is sufficient proof to justify the claim that the brain of people in the ancient times must have been advanced.

CHAPTER 2

HORIZONTAL DIVISION OF THE FACE

DIVISION OF THE FACE ACCORDING TO THE THREE MODES OF MATERIAL NATURE

The face is also divided horizontally into three regions, i.e. the upper zone, the middle zone, and the lower zone. This division is according to the three modes of material nature. Let's have a detailed discussion about the horizontal division of the face according to these three modes of material nature in terms of Vedic face reading.

According to the Vedas, people are divided into the three modes of material nature according to their karma, which is based on their actions in past lives. These three divisions are clearly reflected in the face when it is divided horizontally into three parts. The upper part of the face comprises the upper tip of the forehead to the eyebrows. The middle part of the face constitutes the area below the eyebrows till the nose, and the lower part of the face constitutes the area below the nose to the chin.

The upper zone, also known as the celestial zone represents the mode of goodness. The middle zone represents the mode of passion, and the lower zone represents the mode of ignorance. Through face reading, we can generally find out whether a person is in the mode of goodness, passion, or ignorance. If the upper part of the face is longer than the middle, or the lower parts, then the person is situated in the mode of goodness. If the middle part

HORIZONTAL DIVISION OF THE FACE

RIGHT   LEFT

of the face is longer than the upper and the lower parts, then the person is in the mode of passion, and if the lower part is the longest as compared to the other two parts then the person is situated in the mode of ignorance. However, sometimes we see that all three parts of the face are equal, in that case the person has combined traits of all the three modes. If any part of the face is longer than the other parts, then it should be concluded that the person is predominantly ruled by that mode of material nature. Let us discuss the traits of all the three modes of material nature.

1. The Upper Zone, or the Celestial Zone (Mode of Goodness)

If the upper part of the face, i.e. the forehead, is longer than the middle and lower parts then the person is situated in the mode of goodness. As per the Vedas, people situated in the mode of goodness are purer than others, because this mode is illuminating and frees one from all sinful reactions. People situated in the mode of goodness are conditioned by a sense of happiness. They work on a mental and intellectual plane. These people are not affected by material miseries a lot, and have a sense of advancement in material and spiritual knowledge. These people generally become writers, philosophers, poets, and scientists, or are involved in any field that is related to the mental advancement of a person. The representative types in the mode of goodness as per the Vedas, are the Brahmans in India, who are generally involved in intellectual advancement. These people are generally illuminated by knowledge. People in this category usually follow a pure, healthy diet, free from animal fats, and intoxicants. A person who works in the mode of goodness throughout his/her life, and dies in this mode, attains higher heavenly planets like Heaven.

2. The Middle Zone (Mode of Passion)

People are said to belong to the mode of passion if the middle part of the face is longer than the other two parts. People born in this mode are born with unlimited desires and longings and because of this, whatever they do, their sole purpose is profitable returns, or the desire to have the fruits of their actions. Hence, they are bound to material actions that will profit them in some way. People situated in the mode of passion work on a physical plane. They also live with the bodily conception of life. The person in the mode of passion is never satisfied with the position he/she has already acquired. They eternally hanker to increase their position, power, and bank balance. If a person works in the mode of passion throughout his/her life, and dies in the mode of passion, then he/she takes birth again on earth among people who are eternally engaged and struggling in material activities. The results of actions in the mode of passion are misery, fear, and anxiety. People in this mode are attracted towards a diet that stimulates and which is harsh upon the body.

3. The Lower Zone (Mode of Ignorance)

In this case, the lower zone of the face is the longest, so these people are situated in the mode of ignorance. They madly hanker after sensual gratification in this world without thinking about morality. These people are not even active like the people controlled by the mode of passion, and want everything with minimum effort. Under the spell of ignorance, these people cannot understand things correctly. They are generally not interested in any kind of spiritual understanding. They want to sleep ten to twelve hours a day, or even more, and are addicted to intoxicants. In the mode of ignorance whatever a person does, is neither good for him, nor for others. So the consequences of their activities are good for no one. The results of their activities are usually foolishness, anxiety, tension, and loss of reason. A person who works in the mode of ignorance throughout his/her life, will fall down after death and take birth in the animal kingdom. People in this mode are generally attracted towards professions that revolve around sex, intoxicants, gambling, and other anti-social and immoral activities. The work of those in this category is related to performance without knowledge.

People who are actually serious in this human life generally aspire to reach the mode of goodness with the association of a bona fide spiritual master and transcend the modes of passion and ignorance.

CHAPTER 3

EIGHTEEN SIGNIFICANT POSITIONS ON THE FACE

THE EIGHTEEN SIGNIFICANT POSITIONS ON THE FACE

Just as each country has a map, which provides political, geological, topographical details, likewise our face is also like a map which reveals details about us. However, before looking at any kind of map, there are two basic skills that are important. The first skill is to know how to read the map, and the second is to know the specific regions and the areas related to what we are looking for. The significant positions on the face give details about the regions associated with specific traits. So it is very important to know the whole face. This section deals with the significant positions on the face, and the significance of various positions on the face. Further details about these positions are revealed in chapters that are related to those specific positions.

The First Significant Position: *Region of power and divine consciousness*

1. The Central Axis: The first significant position is the central axis of the forehead. The central axis of the forehead is situated just at the centre of the forehead. So, if we divide the forehead both vertically and horizontally and find the locus exactly in the middle of the forehead then this is the central axis of the forehead. This central axis is a very important position of power on the face, probably one of the most important. This region is

EIGHTEEN SIGNIFICANT POSITIONS ON THE FACE

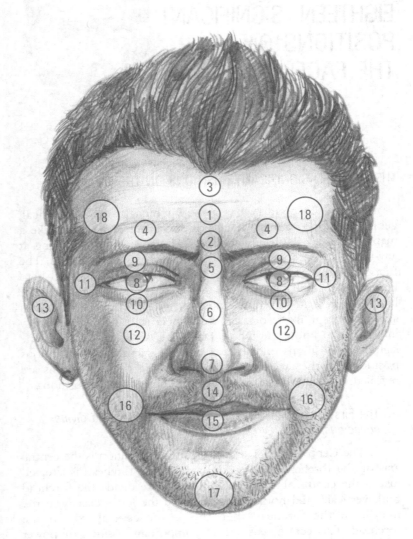

RIGHT   LEFT

also known as the region of divine conscious because this region immediately indicates the exact consciousness of a person. Apart from the divine consciousness, this region also reflects the amount of power a person will possess because all the power, authority, wisdom, and control arises from this place.

This section plays such a dominant role in face reading that it can tell the exact constitutional position of a person. This is such a significant position that it is counted among one of the few positions through which we can easily realise whether the person is born with heavenly qualities, earthly qualities, or with a hellish pedigree. So this section needs to be clearly understood. Further details are revealed in the chapter — lines, in the sub-section — vertical lines and marks on the forehead.

The Second Significant Position: *The Storehouse of power*

2. The Third Eye Region: The second significant position is just below the central axis starting between the eyebrows and is known as the third eye region. The third eye region is known as the storehouse of power on the face as this region clearly reveals how powerful a person is, or will be, in the future. The details are given in the chapter on lines, in the subsection — vertical lines and marks on the forehead.

The Third Significant Position: *The Region of virtue*

3. The Region of Virtue: This position starts at the central axis and ends just below the midpoint of the hairline. This region is the highest region of the forehead and will tell how virtuous and enlightened a person is. This region tells how unbiased and tolerant the person is, how much faith, belief, and confidence a person has and whether the person believes in honesty, integrity and loyalty. How fair and incorrupt a person is, are values and virtue more important for this person, or is there any other material thing that is more important for this person — all this is also represented by this region of the face. Further details are revealed in the chapter — lines, in the subsection — vertical lines and marks on the forehead.

The Fourth Significant Position: *The Regions of fame, wealth, and enjoyment*

4. The Regions of Fame, Wealth and Enjoyment: This region is located just above the eyebrows. The area exactly above the right eyebrow is ruled by the Sun and the area just above the left eyebrow is ruled by the planet Venus. As the Sun is related to glory, effulgence, magnificence, illustriousness, and noble things, similarly, the area above the right eyebrow also gives details about how much glory, fame, or power a person will have in his life and how noble spirited a person is. Again, as the planet Venus is related to beauty, pleasure, enjoyment, sex, luxury, and wealth so the area above the left eyebrow will tell how much the person will be able to enjoy the fruits of labour in his life and what kind of life and enjoyments a person will have in his life and whether the person will really have some pleasure and enjoyment, or if he will have to struggle throughout his life. Full details are revealed in the section — horizontal lines on the forehead.

Again, it should also be noted that this region is also related to siblings, relatives, and close friends. So this region needs detailed assessment, because if this region is inauspiciously built then it will hamper these relationships. Details about this section are also revealed in the chapter — the eyebrows.

The Fifth Significant Position: *The Transition Point between the Mode of Goodness and Mode of Passion*

5. The Transition Point between the Mode of Goodness and Passion: This is a very important area as this is the beginning of the bridge of the nose as well as the transition point from the mode of goodness to the mode of passion. This area ensures a harmonious flow of energies between the two regions. So, the skin in this area should be very smooth and clear. The built of this area is particularly very important because this area gives details about how the person uses his/her wisdom and power for the attainment of various material things like wealth and fortune. Details are revealed in the chapter — the nose.

The Sixth Significant Position: *The physical, mental, and financial structure of a person*

6. The Bridge of the Nose: The bridge of the nose in particular is very important in determining the basic constitution and health of a person. If the bridge of the nose is weak and inauspicious, then this will definitely affect the health of a person and the person will have a weak physical constitution. Further details are revealed in the chapter — the nose.

The Seventh Significant Position: *Character and wealth*

7. The Tip of the Nose: The tip of the nose is the basic determinant of wealth and character. A very auspicious nose is that which is very clear, shiny, and without any marks or clefts. Full details about the tip of the nose, is covered in the chapter — the nose.

The Eighth Significant Position: *Inner power, health, vitality, honesty, and intelligence*

8. The Eyes: The eyes hold the most significant place on the face. The eyes are such a vital asset that if they wouldn't have been present, we wouldn't have been able see or enjoy the beauty of this world and everything would have turned into darkness. In face reading, the eyes are the major determinants of the multiple facets of a person's behaviour, personality, and character. The details about the eyes are explained in the chapter — eyes.

The Ninth Significant Position: *Personal relationships with parents and siblings*

9. The Eyebrows and the area between the Eyelids and the Eyebrows: This region holds a significant position on the face because it reveals a person's relationship with the parents and siblings. A detailed assessment of this region is done in two chapters, i.e. eyebrows and lines. Generally, the moles in different sections in the area between the eyelids and the eyebrows have different meanings, so the assessment of moles will be done in a different chapter on moles.

The Tenth Significant Position: *Family relationships*

10. The area directly below the Eyes: This area is also particularly very important when it comes to revelations about a person's relationship with the family members. Details about this section are revealed in the chapter on lines.

The Eleventh Significant Position: *Sexual relationships*

11. The Corners of the Eyes: The corners of the eyes determine the condition of a person's sexual life, the place given to the wife, mistress, and beloved. This is a very important region in face reading and needs detailed assessment, if a person's sexual nature is to be judged. Details about this section are discussed in the chapter on lines.

The Twelfth Significant Position: *Dominance, aggression etc*

12. The Cheeks and the Cheekbones: The cheeks and the cheekbones are very important when it comes to determining the nature of a person in terms of dominance, aggression, and authority. Details about this section are revealed in the chapter — cheeks and cheekbones.

The Thirteenth Significant Position: *Wisdom and fortune*

13. The Ears: The Ears are the most significant parts of the face, because as the eyes help us see the world, the ears help us listen and understand things around us. Ears are also very significant in face reading, because the ears help us determine the wisdom and fortune of a person. A thorough assessment of each and every facet of the ears is done in the chapter — ears.

The Fourteenth Significant Position: *Sexual appetite*

14. The Philtrum: The philtrum is the fourteenth significant position on the face and tells us about the sexual appetite of the person. It also gives us knowledge about productivity and procreation as well as the physical constitution of a person. Details about this subject are given in the chapter — philtrum.

The Fifteenth Significant Position: *Mindset, personality, nature, sensuality, appetite, wealth, etc.*

15. The Mouth: The mouth is counted as one of the most significant positions on the face. The mouth helps us figure out multiple things about a person because the mouth consists of the mouth as a whole, which includes lips, teeth, tongue, as well as the size and the shape of the mouth. Further details about this section are revealed in the chapter — mouth.

The Sixteenth Significant Position: *Administrative skills*

16. The region of Fa Ling lines: This area reveals the administrative calibre of a person. This region is discussed in detail in the section on Fa Ling lines.

The Seventeenth Significant Position: *Dominance and aggression*

17. The Chin: The chin specifically deals with dominance and aggression. This section is thoroughly explained in the chapter - chin.

The Eighteenth Significant Position: *Travel and movement*

18. Travel and movement: Travel and movement are indicated by the sides of the forehead, just above the corners of the eyebrows. These positions hold a significant place in face reading because these positions help in determining whether a person will have the luck of travelling. These positions also state whether travelling would be beneficial, or will result in losses. Details about this topic are revealed in the section on moles.

It should also be noted that apart from the details given in the specific chapters related to all the eighteen significant positions on the face, details about each and every region of the face is also revealed in the section on moles. So that section should also be carefully reviewed.

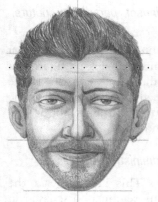

CHAPTER 4

VARIOUS PLANETARY POSITIONS ON THE FACE

Part	Male	Female
Hair	Venus	Venus
Head	Mars	Mars
Right Eye	Sun	Moon
Left Eye	Moon	Sun
Right Ear	Saturn and Mercury	Mars and Mercury
Left Ear	Mars and Mercury	Saturn and Mercury
Nose	Mars	Mars
Mouth	Mercury	Mercury
Teeth	Saturn	Saturn
Tongue	Mercury	Mercury
Cheeks and Cheekbones	Mars	Mars
Jaws	Mars	Mars
Chin	Mars	Mars
Neck	Jupiter	Jupiter
Throat	Venus	Venus
Moles	Mercury	Mercury
Skin	Venus	Venus
Bones	Saturn	Saturn

VARIOUS PLANETARY POSITIONS
ON THE FACE (MALES)

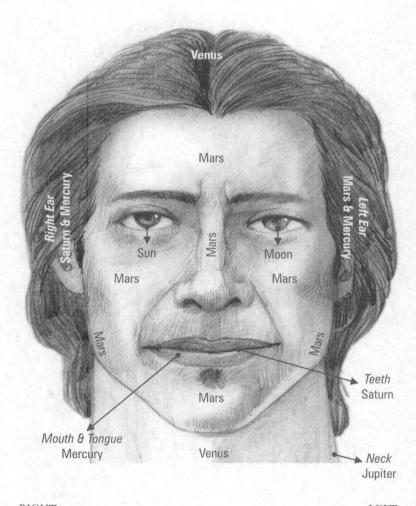

RIGHT   LEFT

VARIOUS PLANETARY POSITIONS
ON THE FACE (FEMALES)

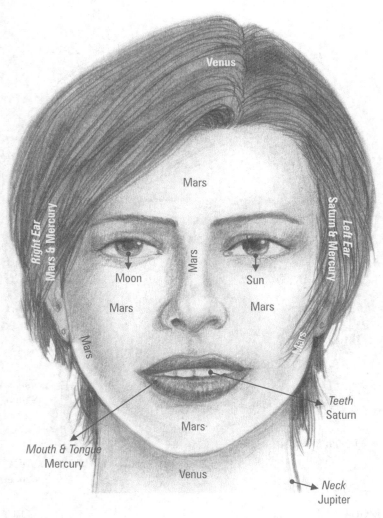

RIGHT   LEFT

CHAPTER 5

THE VARIOUS CATEGORIES AND SHAPES OF THE FACE

THE FOUR BASIC ELEMENTS AND THEIR CORRESPONDING FACES

1. The Earth Type

People in this category generally have longer, more oblong-shaped faces, which are bonier, with a visible jaw line, prominent cheekbones, thickset bodies, sallow complexions, and deep voices. They could be stubborn. According to Vedic physiognomy, earth personalities are also characterised by squarish faces. Earth personalities have the ability to be still, resolute, steady, patient, and firm. They build a solid base in life with their perseverance, patience, and determination. These people are practical, methodical, and deliberate in their outlook and approach towards life, rather than being theoretical. They have the tendency to stretch themselves most of the time to get better results and the tendency to overwork. The forehead should be high and wide as mental direction is important for this elemental type. Earth faces have the energy of growth, potential of seeing the overall picture, and a vision of the future. Earth types with balanced faces are leaders, administrators, and organisers with very strong ideals. They are capable of shouldering lots of responsibility and possess willingness to work for the benefit of others. These people generally have a Mesomorphic, or sometimes an Ectomorphic built.

2. The Water Type

People ruled by the water element are generally sentimental

beings and have short and stocky features. Their facial shapes and body structures are somewhat fleshy. Excessive water in the body gives water personalities round and chubby bodies with soft and plump faces. These people generally possess an endomorphic body. They are also sensitive, gentle and deliberate in their approach, however they like talking a lot which makes them good communicators and story-tellers. So, these people have bright careers in the fields of communication, media, and counselling. Irrespective of the sex, they are predominantly emotional, sensitive, and sentimental, so most of the people falling in this category are prone to weight disorders and emotional difficulties, which means that along with their food, their emotions are not digested correctly.

3. The Fire Type

The fire type has pointed features. They have slightly long, but squarish faces and head, narrow, prominent cheekbones, pointed chin, and a more pointed forehead than those of the oblong type. They are well-built, muscular, and energetic people and generally have Mesomorphic bodies. Fire people have an ardent interest in sports, physical, and outdoor activities because of high energy reserves and solid frames. The fire element brings warmth and enthusiasm to these people's personalities and a capacity to motivate and rejuvenate others. These people are active, goal oriented, fast paced, adventurous and most often, have curly, or wiry hair. Their personalities are characterised by rapid speech and quick body movements. They are very physical in nature and more or less work on a physical plane which makes them very

aggressive, ambitious, and dominating. They are generally very fond of glory, and make capable administrators.

4. The Air Type

The facial structure of air people is generally triangular, or oval, with widely set, chevron cheekbones. Usually good looking, they generally possess fine, soft, or silky hair and have clear, shining eyes that radiate lots of energy. These people are categorised by rational temperaments and usually work on a mental plane, if the other features of their faces are auspicious. They generally possess an ectomorphic body. Air people are very easily recognised by their slender wiry frame, prominent veins in the bodies, and triangular, or oval shaped heads. If these people have high foreheads, i.e. a good

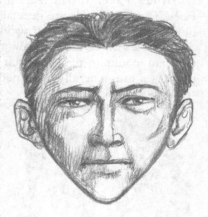

high hairline, then it clearly indicates their excellent intelligence. These people also generally have a huge circle of friends, or colleagues, and they are basically known for their demeanour, and poise. They are also very good listeners. Most of them are very active, quick, versatile, curious, investigative, and are very well suited to areas that need lots of mental exercise and brainstorming.

CATEGORISATION OF FACE ACCORDING TO WIDTH

According to Vedic face reading, faces can also be categorised into two other different categories according to width, or narrowness. Although these faces also belong to one of the four above mentioned elemental categories, this categorisation is generally done because most often people belong to mixed elemental categories and this categorisation helps get a more accurate reading. This makes it easier for people to judge and understand different personalities, according to the temperament that people usually possess, because two people in the same elemental face category might possess different widths, and temperament. For instance, if two people possess 'air' faces, one of them might have a broad face, and the other might have a narrow face, and accordingly they will also possess different temperaments. Similar rules apply for earth, fire, and water faces.

Broad Face: Broad faces are generally wider than normal faces. Their foreheads are generally wider. These faces also might be equal in their height and width, giving a squarish look to the face. These people are generally more tolerant and broadminded than any common person. Their judgment and decision-making processes are generally governed by reasoning and experience.

Because of their high tolerance levels, these people can bear external influences easily, without any problems. These people also have good influencing abilities as they are usually unaffected by external factors like politics, temperature, or bad behaviour and their decision-making process is generally governed by their trust, faith, and authority in themselves. A person with a broad face is also very confident. All these qualities alloyed with a broad-minded outlook makes them good managers. That's the reason you will notice that most of the managers all around the world have broad faces.

Narrow Face: A narrow face is easily noticed because it appears to be thinner than usual. The height of a thin face is greater than its width. The width of this kind of face generally becomes narrow. However, don't get confused between thin faces and oblong faces, because most oblong faces are wider with very wide foreheads. People with a narrow face generally have narrow foreheads as well; however, you won't find all of them having narrow foreheads. These people have a very narrow opinion and view of the world and have very little or no tolerance for people, especially if things do not tend to proceed their own way. This happens because these people are very impatient and might become very anxious, annoyed, or angry even if the slightest pressure is put upon them. Because of this, they might sometimes blow even trivial matters out of

proportion. These people tend to possess zero tolerance levels and are never completely satisfied with anything and always expect more from people and situations.

A narrow faced person might also be very confident by experience, but not by nature. This means that while trying something new, they may feel afraid or anxious. The main challenge for a thin faced person is to overcome the fear that they have within them, because fear is a very big part of their life and if they are not able to overcome this fear, it may make them stick to a certain comfort zone. This can also develop within them the adversity to face challenges and tough situations in life and as a result they might only live an average life. People with these types of faces who also have other inauspicious marks on their face tend to crack under difficult, stressful, and pressurising situations and need constant encouragement to work and develop self-confidence.

CHAPTER 6

MAP OF THE FACE: ONE TO HUNDRED YEARS

MAP OF THE FACE: ONE TO HUNDRED YEARS

This is one of the most important sections in face reading that will enable you to determine age positions on the face, from one to hundred years. In face reading, it is very easy to determine all the major and minor events occurring in a person's life, right from the moment of a person's birth, till the exact time of his/her death. Before proceeding further, a person needs to learn and understand the various areas on the face where different age groups are located. So, we will start with the first year, and then proceed towards hundred. In Vedic face reading however, it should be noted that there are easy techniques to determine the life of a person beyond the age group of hundred as well, but since people in this Age of Kali rarely live beyond hundred years, we will not be discussing this. Again, the one to hundred year age map does not indicate that everybody will live till the age of hundred, as the time of death of each and every individual is different.

Discussed below are the various age groups located in the various areas of the face:

Ages 1-14: The ages one to fourteen are located on the ears, so the luck of a person through these years is seen on the ears. Ages one to seven are arranged systematically from the top to bottom on the left ear, while the ages eight to fourteen are arranged in the

MAP OF THE FACE:
ONE TO HUNDRED YEARS

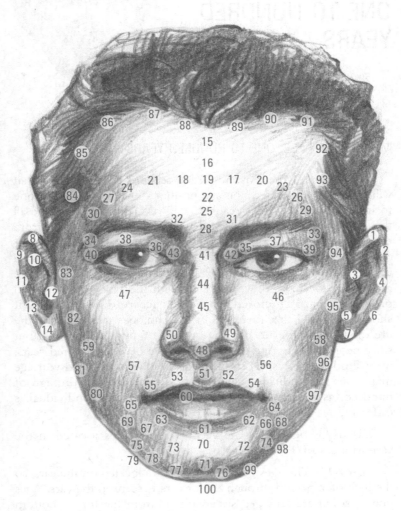

RIGHT   LEFT

same order on the right ear. While determining the quality of life of an individual between the ages one to fourteen, the formation of ears should be considered carefully. If the ears are deformed, then in most cases the person will be born into a family where he/she is not looked after properly by the parents during these ages. It is most likely that the parents will not be well-off. If the size of the ear is very small then in most of the cases it indicates that the period from birth to the age of fourteen will be full of difficulties for this child. However, small ears do not indicate that the person will lack finances throughout life. This person might become very rich, or poor, depending upon his/her deeds and the guidance and company that he/she gets during life. But, most of them turn out to be hardcore materialists, or sensualists, because they want to fill up the gap that has been created during their childhood, by thoroughly enjoying their adult lives.

Ages 15-30: The age group 15-30 is located in the area above the eyebrows, i.e. the entire forehead. Fifteen starts just below the middle of the tip of the forehead, then from sixteen onwards it descends, covering the whole forehead. Age 28 is located in the third eye region, in the middle of both the brows, while the ages 29 and 30 are located on the left, and right temple, respectively. A badly-formed forehead indicates bad memory, low intelligence, and lots of obstacles during these ages.

Ages 31-34: Eyebrows represent the age-group 31-34. For people who are highly artistic and wise with a good temperament, the eyebrows are very even and smooth. However, people who lack good judgement and who are short-tempered, their eyebrows might be inauspiciously built. Eyebrows should not be broken, too sparse, or too thick. Weak eyebrows show tough times in life, while elegant eyebrows indicate a good career, and a good relationship with siblings.

Ages 35-43: Age-groups 35-43 are represented by the eyes and the area around the eyes. The eyes and the area around it should be clear and bright to be included in the auspicious category. If, however, there are dark patches or crisscross patterns there then these people carry a heavy load and disgruntlement. If the eye area is inauspicious then these people will suffer a lot. Some of them might be penalised by the court for some criminal activities. This entrapment by the law usually happens between the ages 35-42.

Ages 44-50: Ages 41, 44, and 45 are represented by the bridge of the nose. Ages 46 and 47 are represented by the cheeks and the cheekbones. Age-group 48 is represented by the tip of the nose, while the ages 49 and 50 are represented by the wings of the nose. If dark patches are present upon the bridge of the nose or upon the cheeks and the cheekbones then the individual might suffer major health problems, especially between the ages 41-47. Dark patches, scars etc. also result in violent changes in relationships. If the nose is crooked, or has dents, then it represents a faulty character and financial restrictions. These people might suffer a lot during the ages 45-50.

Ages 51-73: The age 51 is represented by the philtrum. Age-group 52-55 is represented by the upper part of the lips. Ages 56, 57, 64, 65, 68, and 69 are represented by the Fa Ling lines. In these age groups, the Fa Ling lines have a major impact on ages 56 and 57. Sixty is represented by the mouth, i.e. the lips, while the age-group 61-63, as well as 66-67 are represented by the portion below the lips. Age-group 70-73 is represented by the chin. The well-being of a person between these age groups will depend mostly upon the auspiciousness and inauspiciousness of the placement of these features on the face. Usually, most people die within this period. This mostly happens because of faulty Fa Ling lines, mouths, and chins.

Ages 74-100: These ages are indicated from the sides of the chin going around the circumference of the face, travelling the face in a full circle and coming back down the chin again to complete the full cycle of hundred years. Generally, people do not cross the seventies. Once a person crosses the seventies, especially the seventy-fifth year, then it is time for retrospection for that person. If we observe the circle these ages (74-100) make, we will see that it is in the clock-wise direction, which signifies that if a person has to locate major incidents and happenings within this age group, then they will have to form a symmetry of different ages. It should be remembered that everything in this universe occurs in a very synchronised and systematic way. There is no material element within this universe which is not present within our body. As everything in this universe is systematically placed and all kinds of incidents and happenings (of heavenly bodies in relation to this earth) can be traced by astronomical calculations, likewise all kinds of major and minor happenings within a person's life, right from a person's birth till death, can be calculated by using mystical Vedic techniques. So, a person who is willing to learn and acquire the magical formula should definitely meet a bona fide spiritual master and acquire knowledge in disciplic succession.

While the calculations are done, it should always be kept in mind that the left and the right hand sides (of the face and the body) have different significance for males and females.

PART II

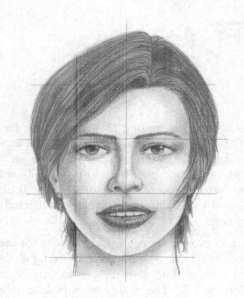

Individual
Facial Features

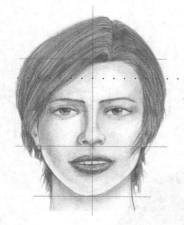

CHAPTER 1

THE HAIR

Venus rules the hair. Among many important facets of one's personality, the hair reflects temperament, sexual inclination, and idea related details. The different types and styles of hair are also associated with one's race, country, and region of birth. Normally, people inherit features according to genetics. The quality of hair is greatly associated with radicalism, revolution, hierarchy, as well as style, and fashion.

Hair varies in colour, diameter, and contour for each and every individual. Individual hair colours vary according to the melanin in them, as well as according to variations in surface structure and distribution of the hair. The quality of hair determines the shape of the hair. For example if the hair is coarse or kinky then it is destined to be shaped like twisted ribbons.

DIFFERENT TYPES OF HAIR

1. Fine, Silky and Straight Hair

Hair that is fine, delicate and silky represents that the Yang forces within are under control. These people display controlled behaviour and even if they get very angry, they won't make their anger very obvious to others. These people have adequate amount of fire element within their bodies and they do not suffer from stomach related disorders.

2. Dry, Rough and Coarse Hair

People whose hair is dry, rough, and coarse have abundant Yang within them. The fire element is not controlled; hence these people suffer from stomach disorders. These people are also very argumentative in nature and they tend to argue over every small detail. If they also have dry lips then they possess wicked dispositions as well. These people tend to suffer a lot in life.

3. Curly Hair

Women with high oestrogen levels and men with high testosterone levels will have curly hair. People with curly hair are very sexual and possess huge sexual appetites. These people are also accustomed to leisure activities. Children with curly hair are mostly interested in outdoor activities, so don't get surprised if you see them grow up to be internationally acclaimed players of some sport.

4. Scattered Hair

Don't mistake this for untidy and uncombed hair. This refers to *hair that grows in different directions*. So this hair does not grow in an orderly fashion. People with such hair will have restless minds; they are never able to focus their mind on any one particular goal or target.

5. Balding

Early balding before the age of 45 indicates the person's weakening constitution. These people are very much inclined towards, interested in, and obsessed with sexual matters. So, the strong sex drive of these people is one major factor that leads to their baldness. The other reason for their early baldness is their impulsive nature. These people get angry very soon and the fits of anger every now and then cause baldness. However, it should be noted that if people become bald after the age of 50 then this shows the development of a spiritual consciousness.

CATEGORISATION OF HAIR ACCORDING TO ITS THICKNESS

1. Thick Hair

Hair that is very thick and strong indicates that the person has a very strong physical constitution. However, these people are basically emotional beings. They might also be very hot-tempered, stubborn, and over-reactive.

2. Thin and Delicate Hair

People with very thin and delicate hair do not have lots of endurance and are also physically very fragile. These people are likely to be more fragile, if their build is slender.

3. Even Thickness/Normal Hair

Normal hair is that which is neither too thin, nor too thick. It is neither too thick or wiry, nor very thin, fragile, and delicate. People who possess hair of even thickness are people with balanced personalities. These people also possess artistic abilities and are very observant in their nature and behaviour.

CATEGORISATION OF HAIR ACCORDING TO DIFFERENT COLOURS AND TEXTURES

1. Black Hair

People with black hair naturally have more melanin in their bodies than their blonde counterparts. It is very important to understand that melanin is a hormone produced by the pineal glands of the body and are formed by cells called melanocytes. Melanin is located in the stratum basal, the bottom layer of the skin's epidermis and in the middle layer of the eye. There are multiple benefits of melanin, for instance, melanin is the mechanism for absorbing heat from the sun, it blocks the ultraviolet rays, protects the skin from cancer and is an anti-aging hormone that prevents wrinkles and other signs of aging. The concentration of melanin in the body is the deciding factor for the complexion of a person.

Melanin is described as a mentally and physically stimulating hormone. So, people with black hair definitely have more stimulants in their hormone than people with blonde hair. Melanin is not only responsible for the colour of the hair, but also the complexion, as well as the colour of the eyes. So, people with very white skin, light hair colour, and light coloured eyes are definitely genetically defective as they suffer from hormonal deficiencies. People who are extremely white, suffer from low melanin, also have freckles, signs of rapid aging, wrinkles, dry skin, cancer etc. Most people who die from skin cancer have extremely white skin. As this book is specifically dedicated to face reading, topics related to skin colour won't be discussed in detail in this book.

2. Red Hair

Red is known as a very dynamic and energetic colour. If the colour of the hair is naturally red, then the person will be high in temperament. If the hair is coloured with red then also the same rules apply, because red hair is a vibrant and dominant colour. However, if a person constantly changes the colour of his/her hair by colouring or dyeing, then this could be the sign of a fickle-minded person.

3. Blonde Hair

As is already stated, lack of melanin causes the hair to look blonde. People with blonde hair are not reluctant to speak their minds, and like being open. These people are direct and sometimes ruthless.

4. Brown/Dark Brown/Tan/Copper

People whose hair colours are brown, dark brown, tan, or copper possess mixed traits of black and red-haired people. These people are more situation-based, especially if their hair colours are naturally of these colours. Some of these people are cunning while others are pragmatic (depending upon their facial traits). This applies both to natural and coloured hair.

5. Mixed Colours

It is not normally seen that people possess mixed coloured

hair, unless they have coloured their hair in different shades. People with mixed coloured hair are indecisive and unsure about most things in their life or about their life and themselves.

6. Blue/Green Colour

Blue, green, or any other shade that is not a natural colour of hair indicates that the person is not afraid of having a completely unique identity of his/her own. These people have different tastes in certain things and they are not scared to make their tastes more obvious to the society.

CATEGORISATION OF THE HAIR ACCORDING TO ITS LENGTH

1. Long Hair

Vedic texts state that Kama resides in the hair and the longer the hair, the greater are the fits of passion. Long hair is also considered to be the sign of royalty, modesty, wealth, and pleasure. The Vedas reveal that women with long hair are blessed with virtuosity, chastity, fortune, and glory. All warriors, princes, and monarchs used to have long hair in ancient India, since this was considered to be the sign of royalty.

2. Short Hair

People with short hair are impetuous. The trend of keeping short hair started in the West and spread across Asia. The monarchs and warriors in the Roman Empire are portrayed with long hair. The first historical mention of short hair was in the portrayal of the Normans and the Knights in the West, most probably during the 11-12th century. The Knights who set off on long campaigns used to cut their hair very short, as this was supposed to be the mark of roughness and impetuosity. Short hair might also have helped them fit their helmets snugly.

CHAPTER 2

HAIRLINE

Wide, smooth and even hairlines are considered to be the best according to Vedic face reading while those that are uneven, jagged, indented, and have bumps are not considered very auspicious. Let's discuss the different types of hairlines and their effects upon the person concerned.

TYPES OF HAIRLINE

1. Even Hairline

People with even hairlines are very even-minded and actually have the quality of being even-tempered and undisturbed in most situations that might disturb a common man. Even hairlines also reveal that these people have had a happy childhood and a non-traumatic adolescence. However, people who have a very even hairline, or an 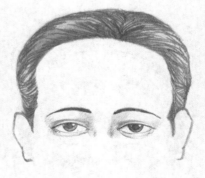 exceptionally even hairline with very thin and soft hair are also very emotional and sensitive.

2. Uneven Hairline

Uneven hairlines are jagged, erratic and faulty. People with uneven hairlines lose their patience very quickly and get irritated very quickly. These people also have the habit of brooding over their past and hence they do not forget bad experiences very easily. They are also not on good terms with their family and friends.

3. Narrow Hairline

People with a narrow hairline like to socialise a lot. These people rarely stay alone and like visiting their friends and partying with them very often. These people also love chatting a lot. So you will always find them being jolly. They are prone to mood swings and are also very sarcastic, but also conform to what others say.

4. Receding Hairline

People with receding hairlines, or a flying hairline, generally tend to get bald between the ages 35-40. People with receding hairlines have impulsive and hasty natures. They sometimes get very restless and like to implement their ideas quickly. These people also get annoyed and angry about trivial issues and usually have a high-pitched voice.

Receding hairlines at a young age indicate a strong sex drive. These people might also take up some kinds of intoxicants like smoking or drinking. However, men with receding hairlines are very fortunate in love.

5. Rectangular or Square-Shaped Hairline

This type of hairline adds width to the forehead and is generally one of the best hairline shapes in terms of luck. People with this type of hairline and forehead shape will have tremendous luck in their studies. People with rectangular or square-shaped hairlines, or foreheads, are also extremely lucky when it comes to receiving the love and attention of their elders and parents.

6. M-Shaped Hairline

If one falls in this category, he/she is a very creative person, interested in the arts, and has a powerful urge to express himself/herself. Almost all the people in the world who possess excellent creativity have M-shaped hairlines. The larger the 'M', the more creative the person tends to be. However M-shaped hairlines are considered to be very masculine so M-shaped hairlines are not considered to be fortunate for women. These women will have lots of difficulties in romantic relationships. Vedic face readers believe that the partners of the women with M-shaped hairlines generally die after marriage.

7. Forehead with Downward Pointed Hairline

In this type of forehead, the hairline points downwards at the centre of the forehead, forming an arch. A person with this type of forehead will work a little harder than others in their adolescent years for increasing their knowledge or skills, or to earn money (perhaps a part-time job to help continue their studies). A pointed hairline shows high intelligence if the hairline is set back and is not too narrow.

8. Crown-Shaped Hairline

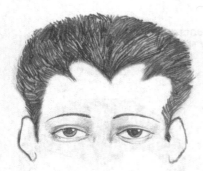

This is another type of downward pointed hairline, however in this type of hairline, the hairline points down at three places, i.e. in the centre of the forehead, and towards the sides, giving the hairline a crown-shaped look. People with this kind of hairline possess unique intelligence and judgement skills. If other facial features are also auspicious, then these people will surpass others with their excellent knowledge, wisdom, and skills. Some of these people who are blessed with other divine features might live life like a king.

9. Peaked Hairline

This is a hairline that rises to a point towards the crown of the head. This hairline is more commonly seen in females. These people are stung by an excessive desire for everything. They are very ambitious and wish to reach prominence in no time. They

also have complete disregard
for the other person's emotions, and are concerned about
their own satisfaction, and
selfish motives. Women with
this type of hairline are also
extremely sexual, so there
are good chances that these
women will get carried away
easily by men who are
very attractive and wealthy.

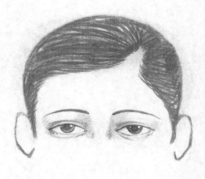

Marriages of most of these women also get delayed. These
people (especially women) are not close to their families as well.

10. Rounded Hairline

This hairline will generally
give a round shape to the
forehead or the face. This is a
watery hair-growth pattern and
water is a changeable element,
so its possessor might possess
a fickle mindset. Also, if the
face shape is round and
connected to the water element
then the possessor of this type
of hair-line will be highly

superstitious and overtly imaginative. However, if people with
other face shapes (apart from the water element) possess this type
of hairline then this hairline will have a positive effect upon the
owner and the person concerned will be highly expressive, with a
charismatic and magnetic personality, as well as strong intuitive
skills.

11. Heart-Shaped Hairline

People with heart-shaped hairlines are extremely sexual,
sensual, and charismatic. You might have observed roadside
Romeos portraying this hairline, as this shape makes the person
more desirable for the opposite sex. Almost all women in
ancient times used to portray this hairstyle, as this made them

appear more obedient to their husbands. According to ancient face readers, people with this type of hairline are known to be wild lovers.

12. Wispy/Patched/Indented Hairline

People with such a hairline are introverts and experts in hiding their emotions. These people are very secretive about everything and will not tell others about their plans and emotions. However, they like getting all the information from others.

13. Strands of Hair Shadowing Down the Forehead

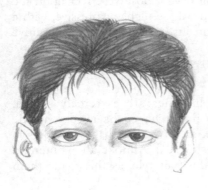

If a person has a hairline such that small strands of hair keep falling on the forehead then the person is very much attracted towards the opposite sex. These people also do not like staying alone and have a strong desire for friends and colleagues, especially for those who belong to the opposite sex.

CHAPTER 3
FOREHEAD

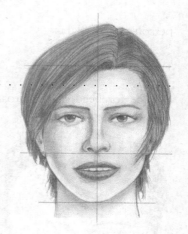

The forehead, as has already been discussed, is the region in the mode of goodness. It is the celestial region of the face. This means that all the heavenly features we receive are indicated by our forehead. The focus here is on our thoughts because we are all the same as human beings, but it is our thoughts that make the difference. It can be easily determined whether the person is intellectual, spiritual, or materialistic, just by looking at the forehead. So, a person who has thoroughly mastered the art of reading can easily tell at which level a person is functioning, just by looking at the forehead.

An individual needs a well-shaped forehead and good eyebrows to be well-endowed with the faculty of logic, memory, and intuition. A well-shaped forehead as described in the Vedic physiognomy is that which is fairly long, evenly arranged, arched, tapering to a point, smooth, rounded and wide. The forehead also needs to be shiny and lustrous and possessing auspicious lines and marks. A shiny forehead tells that a person is destined for success and recognition. People with shiny foreheads become very famous at a certain stage in their life. A forehead that is narrow and shallow reveals a disorganised mind, and untidy thinking. People whose forehead height is less than the length of the nose, or the distance between the tip of the nose to the chin, work either in the mode of passion, or ignorance. As Mars rules the head, so a faulty forehead represents an inauspicious position of Mars in the person's natal chart.

TYPES OF FOREHEAD

The forehead can be broadly categorised as follows:

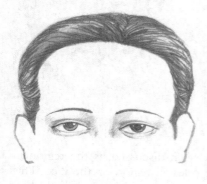

1. High Forehead

A high forehead generally has a higher hairline. People with high foreheads will generally have an easier career path and an easier life as compared to others. A high forehead also indicates high intelligence, power, authority, and aggression. However, it should be noted that a disproportionately high forehead indicates that the person remains in his/her own world unconcerned with social, political, or family issues.

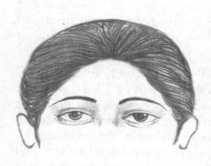

2. Narrow Forehead

If a person's hairline sits low, near the eyebrows, these fore-heads are considered low or narrow foreheads. The corners of this forehead are also much lower and close to the eyebrows, and widens out at the centre, like a staircase. Such a forehead is considered to be an obstacle in the fulfilment of one's ambitions. People with such a forehead are usually low in confidence, and are self-deprecating. They may not have much luck either. They may have encountered money or might have been in a situation where money was more important than studies, however it would be harder for these people to rise to higher positions.

3. Domed Forehead

A rounded hairline produces a dome-shaped forehead. For females, this indicates that she tends to get along with people and does things in moderation. For males, such a forehead signifies that they have high expectations from others, and are picky. They can be stubborn about their career, letting opportunities pass by. A dome-shaped forehead also indicates an absolute love for thrill and excitement.

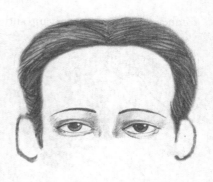

4. Wide Forehead

A wide forehead has good height and width. This is arguably the best shape for one's forehead when it comes to luck. People with such a forehead will have a lot of luck in their studies and are bestowed with intelligence. Their parents and other elders will be able to assist them in their endeavours. This type of forehead is characteristic of someone who likes to take charge and has the ability to run things well when he/she is motivated to do so.

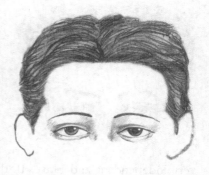

5. Flat Forehead

A flat or straight forehead means that the person is more pragmatic in his approach to life rather than concentrating on theoretical aspects. These people have their own idealistic ways of seeing and doing things. People with flat

foreheads are very observant and analytical.

6. Slanted Forehead

People with slanted foreheads are excited and curious people. These people get excited easily about everything; however their excitement does not last for long. These people often become too conscious about themselves, their status and repercussions and lose interest very often or become introverted, or cautious.

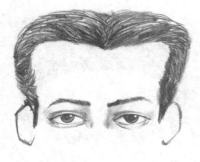

7. High, Round and Deep Forehead

Look sideways at this forehead and you will see a prominent curve extending inwards, on the sides. A person with such a forehead will be very quick paced. Once they make a deci-sion, they will execute it quickly. They are also very independent and brave. If they want to do something, they will do it. They will not hesitate to point out any other person's faults. A high, round and deep forehead depicts idealism, but with a focus on developing strong friendships. These people are certainly ideal as inventors and when it comes to discovering great things. Famous astronauts and scientists generally have such foreheads.

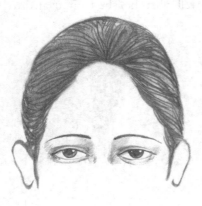

8. Narrow at the Top Forehead

These foreheads are certainly not broad and are

sometimes covered with a thick growth of hair on the sides, giving the forehead a triangular look. A narrow forehead is considered to be an obstacle to fulfilment, especially in social situations and also represents constraints in one's family life.

9. Shallow Forehead

A shallow forehead with a low hairline may cause many obstacles in a person's career and success. It also indicates parental trouble between the ages 15-30. These people generally tend to work very hard and are able to establish themselves only after the age of 30. People with such a forehead generally don't succeed immediately if they are looking for jobs.

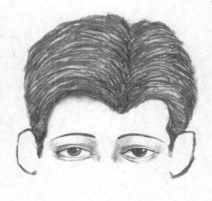

10. Protruding Forehead

Such foreheads are generally protruding and curved in the front, giving the forehead a convex shape. An exaggerated forehead such as this reveals that the person is a dreamer. These people tend to process information step-by-step, very slowly, and do not appreciate being rushed into understanding something new,

or making decisions. They need to anchor their ideas firmly before moving towards achieving it.

11. Indented Forehead

People with indented foreheads are their own bosses, and it's very difficult for them to work under the authority of someone else, or to follow someone else's orders. These people like to be in charge of their own tasks as they are totally independent. They are also hardworking, and therefore will work tirelessly to fulfil their ambitions, dreams and desires without the help of others. So, team work is not really beneficial for them as others tend to take advantage of their hard work and will share the fruits of their labour without making any contribution themselves.

CHAPTER 4

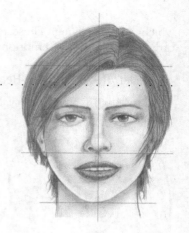

BACK-HEAD

Apart from the forehead, the back-head, i.e. the back portion of the head, is also very important in Vedic face reading. As per Vedic science, the most important areas of the brain are the frontal area, which is right behind the forehead, and the second is the back part of the brain. These two areas are probably the most important areas of human consciousness in the human body. In modern science, these areas have been labelled the association cortex. These areas are more highly advanced and highly evolved than other parts of the brain. So, if one wishes to look at the difference between a genius' brain and that of an average person, then one would look in these regions.

Now let us discuss the types of back-heads in detail:

1. Normal Back-Head

If the back part of the head is normal, i.e. neither flat, recessed, nor protruding, then the person will have an average mindset. These people do not think beyond what they see or perceive. Their beliefs are based upon customs, traditions, and the culture in

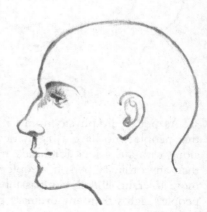

which they are living. These people are just ordinary people with ordinary feelings and emotions.

2. Flat /Recessed Back-Head

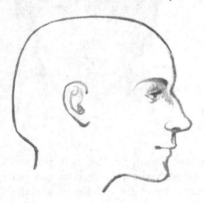

Those who have a very low level of understanding about everything have such a back-head. If you touch the back, or the sides of their head, you will find that the back part, or the sides, are either flat, or slightly recessed. These people are very narrow-minded, conservative, and short-sighted when it comes to understanding something. These are people who search for calamities even in opportunities. They do not trust anyone, as nothing in this world is good enough for them.

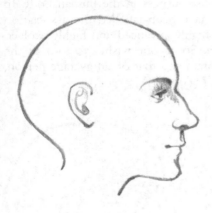

3. Protruding Back-Head

People who have a protruding or fully-developed back-head are the most refined, polished, and sophisticated in all these three categories of back-heads. The most brilliant minds, that ever existed, had protruding back-heads, or a highly developed back part of the head.

As per Vedic physiognomy, it should be taken into account that people who have a highly developed back part of the head, along with auspicious foreheads are definitely superior in wisdom than any ordinary person. People with protruding back-heads are more tolerant, liberal, compassionate, and protective about other people's rights than any ordinary person.

CHAPTER 5
. . . .
EYEBROWS

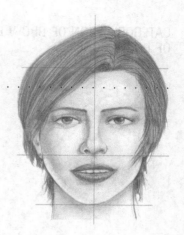

Eyebrows indicate the start of the celestial region of a face. Eyebrows are directly associated with health, longevity, and romance. Eyebrows also represent a person's relationship with one's parents and siblings (especially with siblings). Eyebrows govern the fortunes of a person between the ages 31-34, and can sometimes also indicate one's fortunes till the age of 40. The space between the eyebrows is particularly important. The space between the eyebrows should definitely be thoroughly assessed, as this is the central point of the person's energy and spirit.

BROW BONES

Before discussing the eyebrows, let me briefly explain the significance of the brow bones. Brow bones can tell how aggressive, or submissive, a person is; what kind of physical energy and spirit a person possess; and how exactly a person projects himself in terms of temperament, personality, etc. Brow bones control anger. It can be observed that when people get angry the eyebrows seem strained, and one eyebrow might also be flicked upwards. Brow bones can be divided in two ways, based on the height of the bone, or based on the structure of the bones.

CATEGORISATION OF BROW BONES ACCORDING TO THE HEIGHT OF BROW BONES

1. High-Set Brow Bones

People with high eyebrow bones are usually vigorous and active. These people believe in playing active roles and enjoy having control. These people appreciate power very much and like to wield power themselves.

2. Low-Set Brow Bones

People with low-set brow bones have more controlled emotions. These people also like to take the path of least resistance.

CATEGORISATION OF BROW BONES ACCORDING TO THE BONE STRUCTURE

1. Protruding Brow Bones

If a person has protruding brow bones then this person is aggressive. Protruding brow bones, or protruding bones anywhere on the face, are considered to be characteristically a male trait. Just look at the faces of warriors and soldiers, many of them have protruding brow bones, jaws, chins, as well as cheekbones.

Females with such brow bones are not considered good for homely purposes at all, according to the Vedas.

2. Normal Brow Bones

People with normal brow bones, where the brow bones are not very conspicuous, are people with a normal and controlled temperament. These people will not project a lot of negative attitude in their behaviour. They also do not display their emotions too much in public. These people are best suited for jobs that require intellectual endeavours and controlled behaviour.

3. Recessed Brow Bones

People with recessed brow bones are passive and weak in their constitution, both in their physical energy and spirit. They will not be able to stretch themselves a lot physically, and are not able to handle a lot of physical strain, or pressure. This means that their bodies are highly sensitive and they will feel hurt and pain even at the slightest pressure. They are not mentally very powerful, so a lot of mental pressure and stress might break them down completely.

EYEBROWS

Now, let's discuss in detail, the different types of eyebrows and their effect on an individual.

EYEBROW POSITION: *EYE TO EYEBROW DISTANCE*

Tolerance levels, patience, benevolence, cool-mindedness and an easygoing nature, can all be found out by checking the eye to eyebrow distance. The height of the eyebrows is determined by calculating the relative amount of distance between the brows and the eyes. So, the height of the eyebrows will determine how tolerant a person is, and not the horizontal closeness, or width of the eyebrows.

1. High Eyebrows

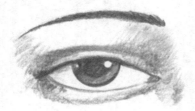

A person with high eyebrows has a lot of vertical gap between their eyes and the eyebrows. Generally, people with high eyebrows live a life of comfort and luxury. These people are very often able to have their own homes within their lifetime, and always benefit a lot from real estate, especially if they are in this business. People with high eyebrows also have very good tolerance levels and are very jolly and fun loving. They are, however, very cautious when it comes to making decisions.

2. Conspicuously High Eyebrows

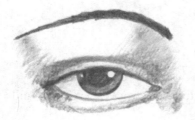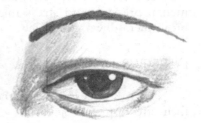

People whose eyebrows are conspicuously high, or higher than normal, are extremely greedy and fickle-minded. They also like to use others to fulfil their own material ambitions, without any regard to human emotions. You will find many women, especially in the glamour industry who have very high eyebrows. These women generally use their sexuality to play with people's emotions and fulfil their material ambitions.

3. Low-Set Eyebrows

Low-set eyebrows are generally those that are very close to the eyes and the vertical gap between the eyes and the eyebrows are negligible. Low-set brows reveal a restless and impulsive temperament. People who have a negligible distance between the eyes and the eyebrows often do things on impulse, in the fit of a moment, and tend to regret their actions later.

4. Middle-Set Brows

These brows are neither too high, nor too low, but are moderately distant from the eyebrows. Their eyelids will not touch or overlap the eyebrows in this case, and both, the eyelids and the eyebrows, are moderately spaced away from each other. These people are always moderate in their temperament. They are neither impulsive, nor do they possess the habit of procrastination, but take only that much time to make a decision as is required by a reasonable person to make a decision.

Middle-browed people often come up with quick ideas and their work never grinds to a halt, or is delayed, if one of their ideas does not work. This is because they are always ready with another idea and keep themselves busy, unless the brows are extremely low-set which will represent a restless nature.

DIFFERENT TYPES AND SHAPES OF THE EYEBROWS

Eyebrows govern desire, activity, and control. It also helps explain the emotions and nature of a person. There are different types of eyebrows, which represent different characteristics and features. The different types of eyebrows and their significance are discussed below.

1. Long Eyebrows

As the eyebrow region represents siblings in physio-gnomy, the length of the eye-brows has a special significance in determining the number of siblings a person will have. If the eyebrows are long, it indicates three to four siblings. Similarly, if the eyebrows extend beyond the eyes, the person concerned is destined to have four to six siblings. However, in the modern age where people generally use medical help to intervene during child birth, or resort to abortion, and other family planning techniques, this prediction could be somewhat inaccurate. In any case, people with long eyebrows will have a larger group of friends than others, and these people will have many admirers.

People with long eyebrows also love beauty and art, especially if the eyebrows are smooth, and not too thick or bushy. These people are very aesthetic in their nature (especially those with smoother and shapely eyebrows) and are very often magnanimous.

These people generally have fulfilling personal and professional lives between the ages 31-34, if their eyebrows are smooth, without any inauspicious marks or dents. Long eyebrows are also related to power, authority, and are deeply connected to wisdom as well. People with larger eyebrows have more magnetism within them than ordinary people and possess very attractive and influential personalities. The larger the eyebrows of a person are; the larger will be the influential abilities of that person. Long eyebrows are also related to longevity.

2. Short Eyeborws

Just as long eyebrows indicate lots of siblings, simi-larly short eyebrows indicate fewer siblings. Short eyebrows also indicate that the person will have more disruptions in their personal and professional lives between 31-34 years. People with short eyebrows could be very rigid at times, and may disregard the consequences of their actions if the other omens on their face represent authority and rigidness.

Vedic face reading also clearly states that short eyebrows are not considered to be a good sign of longevity. Very short eyebrows are associated with poverty and lack of affection from parents and close people during childhood and youth. People with short eyebrows might also become unsuccessful in their amorous relationships. However, if this happens, then these people might turn to violence and criminal activities. People with short eyebrows, which are also thick, are very obstinate and have extreme tempers. Most people with short eyebrows are not able to live beyond the age of fifty.

3. Thick and Dark Eyebrows

People with thick and dark eyebrows are often very warm and friendly as well as very active and agile. These people are however extravagant spenders and believe in showing off. These people will also face hardships during the ages 31-34 (and sometimes till 40), as thick eyebrows indicate a bumpy road ahead, while smooth eyebrows indicate a smooth life between the ages 31-34. However if these people are hardworking by nature, the hard work done between the ages 31-34 will be a good indicator of Karmic rewards in the later stages of life, and will be an essential learning period for later events.

It should be noted that thick, dark, and long eyebrows are associated with strength, courage, tolerance and other positive attributes. So, if a person's eyebrows are thick, long, and dark then the individual's life forces are powerful. These eyebrows are clear indicators of longevity, good health, and wisdom. If a person has long, thick, and dark eyebrows coupled with hair in the ears then this is regarded as the most dependable signs of longevity. However, others who have short and sparse eyebrows are susceptible to illnesses and have a short and limited lifespan, as well as limited wisdom.

The appearance of one or more grey hairs in the eyebrows (for all kinds of eyebrows) during one's youth is a clear warning that the person will have bad health in the future. This person will regularly suffer from health-related problems since the hair of the eyebrows is the last to turn grey. Women with conspicuously thick eyebrows are believed to be capable of bearing many children.

4. Bushy Eyebrows

If the eyebrows are very thick and bushy then this is the sign

of a rigid, intolerant, and inflexible person. If these eyebrows are close to the eyes then these people will also be prone to anger and violence. If these eyebrows join in the middle then this indicates some kind of inner conflict, which throws the person into anger and despondency every now and then. Generally, people with very thick eyebrows are not great intellectuals and lack wisdom and resources. These people generally face a lot of trouble when establishing themselves in life. Most of them are able to find a decent job only during their middle years, mostly by the age of 35, so these people are advised not to marry until their early, or late, thirties.

5. Thin or Sparse Eyebrows

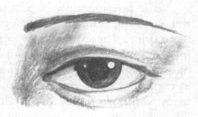

Women with sparse and thin eyebrows are very fickle-minded, unsteady, restless, and agile. Thin eyebrows are generally a symbol of beauty, especially for women. That's the reason why most women use artificial means to make their eyebrows look thinner.

Women with light and sparse eyebrows make good assistants, cabin crews, sales women, nurses etc. These women are more detail-oriented and follow directions correctly. They also make good models, or work in professions where there is a need for more activity. Light or sparse eyebrows are also indicators of a person's inclination towards sex and sensuality. Men with such eyebrows are also suited for acting, or any art-related profession, since these eyebrows produce positive vibrations for the lovers of beauty and art. They could also involve themselves in sports, or other fields that require more activity.

6. Pencil-Thin Eyebrows

Eyebrows that are pencil thin, high, and round reflect a deeply sentimental person. These people are oversensitive, and constantly need reassurance. These people, especially if the subject is a woman, are highly sexed as well, and their bodies are more sensitive to external stimulus as compared to other women. They have very delicate and soft features which are sensitive and respond to pain, and pleasure very quickly.

Vedic physiognomy is of the opinion that people with very thin, round, and high i.e. crescent shaped eyebrows are ingratiating. These people are very clever and manipulative. Both men and women who possess crescent-shaped eyebrows are great pleasure seekers. Men with such eyebrows very often get involved in conflicts because of their attraction towards women. There are many women in the glamour industry, such as actresses or models, who subconsciously give a crescent-shape to their eyebrows because it increases the sexual strength of women and helps them project themselves in a more sexual and appealing manner to the audience, especially the men.

7. Fading Eyebrows

As discussed in the section on short eyebrows, fading eyebrows are not considered to be good for the destiny of a person irrespective of whether the eyebrows are thick or thin. Eyebrows represent one's thought process, wisdom, and intellect, because of its presence in the celestial region of the face. People

who possess fading eyebrows could be ambitious to the extent of madness. These people do not possess humility and kindness. Most of these people lack proper judgement and direction in life. Because of lack of judgement, direction, and self-control, most of these people are tyrants, robbers and criminals. The only things that these people are obsessed with are money, pleasure, and power.

8. Straight Eyebrows

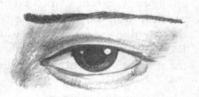

Straight eyebrows are those that are straight and horizontal without any curves. People with straight eyebrows generally possess assertive personalities. Straight eye-browed people are also very rigid in their way of thinking and code of conduct. These people stand for no nonsense. If you want to convince them about something, then you must only use logic and show them proof. Don't try to convince them just by using emotions. These eyebrows are also called masculine eyebrows because people with these eyebrows are overtly masculine in nature.

Vedic physiognomy is of the opinion that these eyebrows are not at all good for women. These women possess zero tolerance level, and they never take the backseat. They could also turn very revengeful, if they have made up their mind to harm you. They are neither flexible nor forgiving. As per Vedic face reading, for all other eyebrow types, closely spaced eyebrows represent the concentration powers of a person, however for straight eye-browed people (especially women), this represents lack of tolerance.

9. Round Eyebrows

Round eyebrows are those which make a half-round shape above the eyes like an angular moon. These eyebrows are compared with the moon, so they indicate a person filled with emotions. Crescent-shaped eyebrows in women indicate an innate physical urge for sex. People with round eyebrows, especially if they are thin are more prone to fantasies, and like living in dreams. People with moon-shaped eyebrows generally have a good chance for promotions, between the ages 31-34.

10. Curved Eyebrows

If the eyebrows of a per-son curve in such a way that they are similar to a cat's eye, then the person tends to be an opportunist. Women whose eyebrows generally slant upward and then take a steeping downward curve tend to be extremely self-centred and opportunists. They generally use their body and skills to gain victory over people and situations just by playing with people's emotions and weak points.

11. Brows with the Tail Pointed Upwards

These brows have their ends pointed upwards at the edge of the face. These eye-brows are indicative of a person working on a meta-physical or spiritual plane. People with such eyebrows work in the mode of goodness and possess all the qualities possessed by the people in this mode. These eyebrows are considered to be an indication of an eternal optimist. These people are generally visionaries and work towards their vision with unflinching determination. They are self-motivated and are determined to achieve whatever they want in life. These people generally have very strong work ethics and will expect the same from others.

These eyebrows also indicate pride and honour. These people generally demand a lot of respect. These eyebrows sometimes also indicate courage and conflict as these eyebrows were generally possessed by great warriors in ancient times. So other facial features should be thoroughly assessed in people possessing these eyebrows.

12. Broken Eyebrows

 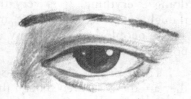

People whose eyebrows are generally broken in the middle since birth or because of some scars or accidents, fall in the category of broken brows. If a person has such disrupted brows, it generally indicates that the person will have a difficult life ahead. These people generally face disruptions in their career path and personal lives especially during the ages of 31-40. Broken, or disrupted eyebrows, also indicate that the person will have a bad and unhealthy relationship with his/her parents and siblings, or other relatives. This also indicates that a sibling might have passed away early in their life, or in some cases, one or both of the parents might have passed away. If there is a crossing crease dividing the brow into two parts then the person needs to be careful, as there might be a life-threatening accident in his/her life, which might result in death.

13. Arched or Angled Eyebrows

Arched eyebrows are generally also called angled eyebrows as these eyebrows give an angular shape to the eyebrows. Arched eyebrows are like an inverted 'v', with a chevron (point) at the top of the brow. Arched eyebrows signify a person who has a dominant, assertive, and aggressive personality, who is always willing to seek control, and authority. These eyebrows also indicate that these people enjoy being unique and they prefer marching to the beat of their own drum and have a unique way of doing everything. It is very difficult to change their habits, thoughts, beliefs, personality, methodology, and style of work. These people become happy and motivated when they have power and control.

These people always choose the best things and think that they are the best, even though they may lack many things. Greatly arched V-shaped eyebrows are characteristic of people who won't hesitate to use people's emotions to gain whatever they want in life. Success comes easily for these people, as most people with arched eyebrows become successful or famous before the age of thirty.

14. Tangled Eyebrows

These eyebrows are thick, bushy, and tangled. These eyebrows can be easily identified on the basis of the curls encircling the brows at different points. These people do not easily trust others and will test you in every possible way, to their own satisfaction. These people themselves are complicated human beings, but like to test others by taking the stance of a devil's advocate.

Curled and tangled eyebrows also indicate that the personal relationships of these people are not strong with their parents and siblings. Sometimes these people are also on the verge of breaking up some personal relationship. It also indicates that the person concerned will struggle and have many bad influences around him/her between the ages 31-40.

15. Winged Eyebrows

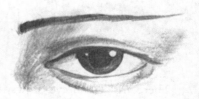

People who are visionaries have winged eyebrows. These eyebrows are shaped as the wings of birds taking flight. These people are generally farsighted. They are generally scholars, or masters, in their subject. They generally become successful because of their sharp minds and intellect.

16. Asymmetrical Eyebrows

In this category each eyebrow is of a different shape or size and is therefore called asymmetrical. These eyebrows indicate a very big contrast between the mind and heart of a person. People with asymmetrical eyebrows possess complicated personalities and it is very difficult to guess their future course of action. Their actions always shock their colleagues and people who know them. They are definitely not balanced and will have a difficult life, especially between the ages 31-40. If these eyebrows are joined in the middle then these people will suffer a heavy blow of fate, and it will be difficult for them to re-establish themselves.

17. Brows curved upwards in the Beginning

There are certain eye-brows that make an upward curve at the start of the eyebrows. These eyebrows are considered to be very unlucky for the person who possesses them. People with such eyebrows are generally fanatics. They have extremely low tolerance levels. They tend to get angry very soon and sometimes possess a cruel nature. Generally, these eyebrows indicate a violent nature. People with such eyebrows are short-tempered and tend to blow up trivial matters way out of proportion.

18. Downward Sloping/Weeping Eyebrows

Downward sloping eye-brows are also called weeping eyebrows because when people cry, most of them scrunch their eyebrows down. People with weeping eyebrows portray the same characteristics portrayed by people who are experiencing chronic grief. Their eyebrows are such that people pity them. Since people tend to assume that such people need pity and compassion, people with such eyebrows tend to benefit from the favour others bestow on them. However, these people might not be very friendly with others. If the subject is female, she will like to depend upon others, especially upon her spouse for her bread and butter. Both the sexes falling in this category do not like to do a lot of physical labour.

EYEBROW-SPACING

1. Closely-Set Brows

Brows that are generally closely set together reveal very unique concentration powers. These people are hardly, or not at all, disturbed by noises and disturbances when they focus upon anything. They also have the power to go deep into a particular thing, or situation. However, their eagerness for details is restricted only to things in which they are interested, otherwise they do not show much interest in things that are not of their interest.

2. Widely-Set Brows

Widely-set brows that have a clean and clear space between them are generally regarded as the philosopher's field of activity, unless the brows are very widely set apart. To be considered in the category of wide eyebrows, the person's eyebrows should have only one vertical eye gap between both the eyebrows, as that is the ideal distance between the eyebrows. These people are very unique when it comes to having deep knowledge, and a great understanding of the world. They possess an even temperament. They are very deliberate in their actions and work on a deep mental plane. They possess a thinking mind and generally love mankind, and like working for mankind. Their philosophical temperament generally makes them apt philosophers, poets, or writers. These people are also very tolerant towards others and generally do not get affected by the vicissitudes of fortune. Their minds are constantly focused upon creating something new.

If the gaps between both the eyebrows are even slightly more than one vertical eye gap, then the eyebrows are said to be very widely set apart. It should be noted that the eyebrows which are very widely set apart are not considered to be very auspicious. These people tend to be very indecisive most of the time. They are always in a dilemma about their decisions, and mostly take the wrong decisions and tend to regret it later. People with very widely set apart eyes or eyebrows tend to procrastinate. These people tend to move in a very unrealistic world. They might also become dreamers and waste their life and time just thinking and speculating without ever applying their thoughts into action.

3. Eyebrows Joined in the Middle

If the left and right eye-brows are not clearly separa-ted, but are joined in the middle with a bridge of hair, then this means it is joined in the middle. Sometimes, the joining of the eyebrows in the middle is very thick and clear. Eyebrows that are joined in the middle of the eyes represent a galaxy of symptoms/phenomena.

A detailed description about the traits of the people with joint eyebrows is given.

I.   These people are worried about each and everything in their life. Even small and trivial issues bother them very much. Their minds are always on the go and it is very hard for them to relax, since they think all the time. They think about useless and trivial matters and are very often anxious. Their future prospects also bother them a lot and they are always thinking about how they can secure their future.

II. As these people think a lot, they think they are great intellectuals (especially the women) and have the habit of interfering in everything, because they want to correct everything. As spouses also they tend to be very controlling. They will never take the back seat and will keep on offering useless suggestions and would like to control everything.

III. These people have the habit of taking everything very personally. Anything and everything referred to in their presence is meant to be taken personally. They (especially women) always see themselves as being taken advantage of, insulted, and disrespected. This distresses them and they develop a retaliating attitude.

IV. These people are very cautious in their code of

conduct as they want to present themselves as people of great character. Especially women with such eyebrows are very serious about how the world sees them. They are always engrossed in thinking about what the other person might think about their character. Hence, these people are always afraid.

V. The above reasons being the causes of their actions, these people, especially women, tend to become very secretive and try to keep secrets from their husbands and parents out of fear, especially if they are having an amorous relationship, or an affair with any man. Even while speaking to a male classmate, or colleague, these women become very restless and cautious if someone is around. These women start thinking about what the others are thinking.

VI. These people (especially women) tend to be very defensive about everything. They don't realise that it is their own edgy attitude, way of thinking, and provocative nature that initiates strife.

VII. Eyebrows meeting in the middle also indicate that the person is not sure of anything, is very confused, and uselessly cautious about the decisions he/she makes.

VIII. Eyebrows meeting in the middle indicate karmic reactions from previous births. As per Vedic face reading, these people have to bear the fruits of their previous lives and bad deeds in this life. This also indicates a severe blow of destiny or fortune in this life. It indicates that the person will have to struggle through life to learn the basic fundamentals of life. Generally, these people do not have the best luck before the age of 30, unless they are born in a rich and intellectual family, or are working under the guidance of a powerful person. If some other good omens are not present in their natal charts, these people will have a bumpy road ahead, and all their efforts might be in vain.

IX. It is also believed that when people with eyebrows meeting in the middle are born, they take away the life of some other person in their family. This might happen if there are no good omens in their natal chart.

Also people whose eyebrows meet in the middle are not auspicious for their relatives, siblings, friends and acquaintances who stay with them, or who are related to them, as these people somehow bring ill fortune to their associates as well. However, all these cases should also be very precisely calculated with their horoscopes at the time of their birth, under the guidance of a bona fide spiritual master.

X.   As the hair covers the space between the brow which is the region of the third eye, which is generally considered to be the focal point of a person's spiritual powers, energy, and spirit so people with joint eyebrows lack will-power and guts, and might become very introverted, shy, hesitant, self-deprecating, or in extreme cases, this might result in envy, resentment, hatred, revenge, and jealousy which they experience when they see the progress of siblings, friends, and colleagues. As the brow covers the region of the third eye so this also affects their mood and behaviour and they are prone to immediate mood swings, become indecisive, and unsure about everything, including their own feelings.

XI.   These people develop a habit of fault-finding once they have started the act of self-deprecation, and if they are miserable. They do not tend to compromise or learn from their past (unless some of them are at a higher level because of the presence of other good omens in their natal charts).

XII. These people always keep their preferences at top priority. They always judge a relationship by calculating how much they receive and not by how much they wish to give or contribute to the relationship. If the person with eyebrows joint in the middle is a woman, she will definitely see how much the man who is in love with her, loves her and what facilities he can offer her. Whether she loves him or not, or whether she is capable of contributing something to him will be secondary, and of no concern to her.

XIII. People with joint eyebrows are extremely unforgiving

(especially if the subject is a woman).

XIV.   They are very narrow-minded and conservative, to the extent of lacking tolerance and have extremely low tolerance levels.

QUALITATIVE DIVISION OF THE EYEBROWS

Apart from the above division which was related to the different types of eyebrows which determined specific characteristics, the eyebrows are also further divided into four more categories, according to the distribution of hair in the eyebrows. These qualities are often described by the way in which a person tends to look at a particular work and project and the way one's emotions and intellects are shaped through the project. Let us take an overview of these three categories of eyebrows as well.

I. Thick at the start

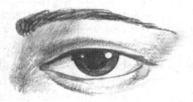

For such eyebrows, the hair is generally thicker at the start and becomes thinner as it moves towards the end. People with such eyebrows are generally ideal when given idea-related projects, as their minds are very sharp and full of new ideas, and concepts. These people often possess proper mannerisms, and are very cultured as long as other inauspicious signs are not present on their faces. Because of their enthusiasm and keen interest, they take up new projects and dedicate their whole energy towards the completion of that project.

II. Even eyebrows from beginning till the end

These eyebrows are even in thickness right from the beginning

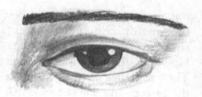

till the end. Most of such people possess even temperaments. They do not like being rushed into decisions and take their own time to make decisions. These people will not give a lot of ideas as they do not believe in unnecessary distribution of knowledge, or ideas, and speak only when they think it's necessary to do so. They also will not show an avid interest in your ideas and will take their time to reach their decision about starting a project. However, once they become interested in a project, or take up an idea, they will work constantly with the same passion and determination with which they began the task. As these people fall in the middle category, they are certainly good in brainstorming sessions as well. These people are moderate when it comes to handling monotony and high-pressure situations. However, these people are not as active and agile as people with eyebrows thick in the beginning and will work at a mediocre pace to complete their tasks.

III. Thick in the end

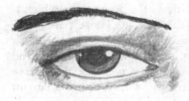
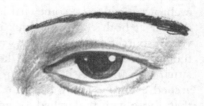

Now, let's come to the third category which is quite opposite to the first category. These eyebrows have a thin-ner beginning and thicker end. People in this category are generally ideal when dealing with control-related projects. So, these people generally do not like new ideas popping up every now and then, and resist any kind of change unless absolutely necessary. These people will also not show an avid interest in new ideas and concepts until they are thoroughly convinced. They are very slow, or probably the slowest, when it comes to taking up a new idea or project. However, these people are quite good in following-up on tasks. They will stick to the project with full force from the middle of the project and will see to it that the project is completed nicely in the end.

These people thrive on being involved in all details and hence, you will find them in every brainstorming session. However, these people like keeping everything under their control, so people who are looking for space in relationships or jobs might feel choked with them. So, only those who like working under strict supervision and disciplinary officers can work under these people.

IV. Thick in the middle

These eyebrows are gene-rally thin in the beginning as well as thin at the end, but thick in the middle. The shape of these eyebrows tends to be somewhat like that of a boomerang which is thinner at both ends, but thick in the middle. These people are very resourceful and generally work as proprietors of a particular thought or idea. They are very keen about controlling people and situations and possess the same qualities as those who have arched eyebrows. However, these people will be more adamant than those with the arched, or angled eyebrows. These people do not get excited at the start of a project, nor when it is over, but are interested in the results. They are generally motivated by the idea of making a profit. However, if these people do not learn to examine the projects in detail and their outlook towards it, they might have to face losses in the long run. These people are also very narrow-minded and rigid, so their narrow-mindedness, conservativeness and rigidity might become a hindrance if flexibility is required. These people are never able to relax because of their nature.

While reading the facial features it is very important that the face reader should generally do a detailed analysis of the type and exact shape of the eyebrows, as well as match the qualitative division of the eyebrows and then conclude which category the subject generally falls into. A detailed analysis of all the aspects gives a better insight about the person's personality, character, inclinations, and destiny.

SOME OTHER FEATURES OF THE EYEBROWS

1. Different length, shape, and position of the eyebrows

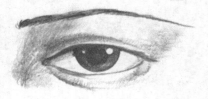

The different length, shape, and positions of the eyebrows, i.e. one eyebrow being longer, higher, or straighter than the other, means that the person might have more than one father. In some cases, the person's mother might die and he/she might have to accept a step-mother. In some cases, the mother or father might have many extramarital affairs. If the mother is having an extramarital affair, she will not be able to determine who the father is. In some cases, these people tend to have mothers who are prostitutes. In addition to all this, these people's fortune will always be turbulent and they will mostly have to struggle through their lives. This will be more so if other omens on their faces, or body, are not good. These people will have to go through a lot of hardships, especially between the ages 31-34, or till the age of 40.

2. Big Mess

If the eyebrows seem like a big mess then this person is definitely not good with money matters. These eyebrows

represent a huge financial loss. This bad condition will be worse if the nostrils are flared and the hair in the nostrils is clearly visible.

3. Curling Brows

If the hair of the brows curl, making a full, or half circle, then these brows indicate a bad relationship with parents and siblings. These eyebrows also indicate a struggle when the person is 31-40 years old.

4. People with beautiful and well-defined brows

Beautiful and well defined brows are those that are naturally shaped very nicely. These people are full of ideas and creativity and tend to choose a creative and artistic field. These people definitely become good writers, poets, historians, trend setters, artists, and superstars.

5. Eyebrows with vertical growth of hair

Normally, if we look at any eyebrow, we will see that the hair in the eyebrows slants horizontally, however the hair might grow vertically in some cases. People with such eyebrows are tenacious. These people never give up, no matter what obstacles they might have to face.

6. A crossing crease, or a line in the middle of any eyebrow

If there is a clear crease or a line in the middle of any eyebrow, crossing or dividing the eyebrows, then the person will have a life-threatening accident in his or her lifetime. If the other omens are not good then this can lead to the person's death.

7. Two or more creases on the eyebrows

Two or more creases on the eyebrows indicate the subject's separation from the parents. This might be due to a divorce, death, or family conflict. People with two or more creases on the eyebrows will have to struggle before the age of 28, and will not have the best luck before that age.

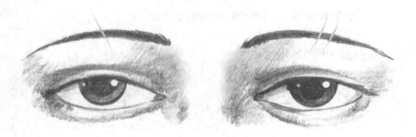

8. Noticeable hair between the eyebrows

Even if the eyebrows are not joined and there is some hair between the brows which is clearly noticeable, this indicates that the person will not have family riches, and will have to struggle a lot to make or earn a fortune. The best time for them also starts after the age of 30.

9. Change in colour of the eyebrow

If the colour of the eyebrow changes (when in contact with sunlight, or otherwise) and turns slightly yellow or brown, it is an indication of good luck in the near future in the person's professional and personal life. A purple hue represents deep love for someone. It is an indication of a person falling in true love with someone. A red hue indicates danger and grave troubles in the near future, as well as an obstruction to progress. A green hue on the eyebrows indicates that the person will be troubled and let down by someone at work. If the hue is darker than the eyebrows (probably black) then it indicates a disaster in the near future. Apart from other age groups, the colour of the eyebrows should be very clearly judged when the person is 30-35 years old.

CHAPTER 6

EYELASHES

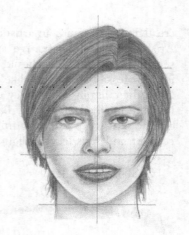

Eyelashes are one of the important parts of the face. Most face readers ignore many parts of the face, including the eyelashes. These face readers are not aware that everything in this world comes in a package, whether it is a person's body, face, or anything else. Like I stated earlier, the face is a map and if the face reader who is involved in face reading omits a particular section then that face reader is viewing an incomplete map.

Eyelashes can be generally categorised as:

1. Long Eyelashes

Long Eyelashes   Side view of Long Eyelashes

Long eyelashes are generally possessed by very creative, artistic, and sensitive people. These people possess very creative and thoughtful minds; therefore professions that involve a lot of creativity and require an artistic approach are best suited for them. Apart from being creative and artistic, these people are very sensitive as well. So, it should be taken care that these people get into professions that they like, because if they do not get support from their family when they choose a profession towards which they are inclined, or if they have to get into any other profession due to unfavourable circumstances then they might not feel content and satisfied throughout their lives.

2. Short Eyelashes

Short Eyelashes   Side view of Short Eyelashes

Short eyelashes are generally possessed by those who are practical beings. These people are unconcerned about what profession they are involved in, as long as there is a continuous flow of money and they have some advantage by being in that profession. They also do not try to use their own creative skills. They use techniques that someone else has already successfully experimented with. These people do not like to lose their energies until and unless it is certain that they are benefited in some way.

3. Thick and Strong Eyelashes

Thick and strong eyelashes are generally possessed by those who are very energetic, industrious, strong-willed, and hardworking. These people will also be very healthy, so they will rarely fall sick. If the eyelashes are long and strong then these people will remain strongly focused towards their specified goals and targets because apart from being energetic, perseverance is innate.

4. Thin and Weak Eyelashes

If the lashes are so thin and weak that they easily break, then the person concerned does not have a strong constitution. These people fall sick very easily. They are also not very hard working and tend to be lazy and sluggish.

5. Dark Eyelashes

Dark eyelashes are considered to be a symbol of eroticism. In ancient India, it was considered that women whose eyelashes were big and dark were very erotic and sexual. It was also considered that these women are very sensitive to the sense of touch and that they understand the language of signs very easily.

6. Light Eyelashes

People with light eyelashes lack sex appeal and vigour.

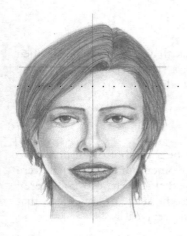

EYES

Eyes certainly rule the face and are the windows to one's soul and secrets. The eyes tell the world how powerful, or trustworthy a person is. Powerful eyes are able to assess other people and situations more accurately than those with submissive, weak, or watery eyes. Good eyes that are clear, prominent, and shiny with a bright sparkle or glitter, indicate that the person is confident, strong-hearted, trustworthy, lacks inner stress, is reliable, and confident. Small, squint, or shifty eyes always reveal faint-heartedness, an introverted, or secretive nature.

A steady gaze determines the forthright disposition of a person. It also reflects that the person is honest, hardworking, solid, persevering, stable, introspective, and is a deep thinker. This is in contrast to wandering or shifty eyes, which portray unsettled and inconsistent habits. One's eyes are ruled by the Sun and the Moon in Vedic physiognomy, so auspicious eyes represent the auspicious placement of the Sun and the Moon in the natal chart.

TYPES OF EYES

As per Vedic physiognomy, eyes are divided into different categories according to their types, features, spacing, colour (or hue) of the eyes (the irises), different marks and signs on the eyes etc. In this section, we will discuss in detail the different types of eyes and the qualities associated with them.

1. Lotus Eyes

This is the most important eye type. Lotus eyes are generally large and wide and prominently resemble lotus petals. This category includes the eyes of the Supreme Personality of Godhead Sri Krishna, or his plenary expansion, Vishnu. This eye type indicates virtue and people possessing these eyes generally work on the intellectual and spiritual plane and possess all the mystical qualities that situate them in a transcendental position. These people possess high intuitive powers and have tremendous capabilities of organising and administering things. Such eyes also indicate the person's dexterity and eloquence. These people are generally very good at delivering public speeches without any fear and possess excellent leadership qualities. They also possess the ability to see and judge each and everything from multiple perspectives to ascertain the credibility of an object, person, or situation. They are quick in making decisions, and excellent in brainstorming and envisioning things.

The general features of these eyes are that they are wide, shiny, crystal clear, and firm in their gaze. The eyelashes are beautiful, black and big. People with such eyes rarely blink while gazing at a particular person, or object. They make excellent scientists, poets, writers, politicians, businessmen, filmmakers, musicians, actors, and artists, and such people are excellent in intellectual fields.

2. Deer Eyes

These eyes resemble that of the deer and are extremely beautiful. These eyes are large and wide with pointed corners and big eyelashes. The eyebrows are very thin and well-shaped. These

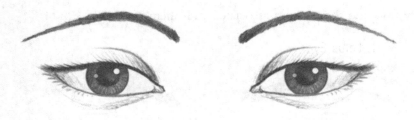

eyes are very sensual, erotic, and full of desire for love and sexual feelings. Women possessing such eyes are very beautiful and sexy and generally have roving eyes, searching for a person who can share their physical longings. These women feel restless and uneasy if they do not have a satisfying sexual life. Men in this category possess flirty dispositions, and both men and women who fall in this category possess soft features. These people can do well as models, or in the field of advertising, media, and acting.

3. Round and Small Eyes Resembling a Fish

Just take a close look at these eyes. These eyes are round and small and resemble the eyes of a fish. People possessing such eyes are extremely selfish and are opportunity seekers who fulfil their desires without giving any importance to moral considerations. If people with such eyes also seem shifty-eyed, then beware. Such people could be extremely dangerous and revengeful, even for the smallest reason, especially when their desires are not properly fulfilled.

4. Big Eyes/Large Eyes

These eyes are larger and bigger than most eyes and are very beautiful and sexy looking. Generally, it is seen that most successful models and actresses have big eyes. Women with such

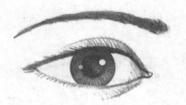

eyes are also considered to be very sexy and sensual like those possessing deer eyes, however these women are not as shrewd as those who have deer eyes. These eyes indicate an outgoing and outwardly nature. These people are generally extroverts, however, they need a chance to mingle and only then do they speak, otherwise they prefer to keep their mouth shut when they are in a crowd.

Men with large eyes usually attract lots of beautiful women towards them as they are very attractive and pleasant to women. These men are also very conspicuous, artistic and full of spirit. These men are generally involved in revolutionary projects as they tend to be attracted by radical thoughts, speech, and actions. This eye represents a well-deserved karmic reward. Like the lotus-eyed men, men with large eyes are an epitome of beauty and refined behaviour. They start out in life with a big advantage. Among all the categories, the lotus eyes, bull's eyes, and large eyes are considered to be the three most superior category of eyes, (especially lotus eyes and bull's eyes because these eyes are generally big as well).

Girls born with large eyes are also considered very special, are loved, admired, and pampered by everyone. The special treatment continues and by the time they reach their teens, a large number of men and women start getting irresistibly drawn towards them. As large-eyed girls have better luck than other women, most of them who are clever use the emotions of others, to reach their goals.

People who have large bright eyes, dark eyebrows and swarthy facial features are very aggressive, powerful, and are able to reach the position of power and authority by the age of 35-40.

5. Trance Eyes/Bull's Eyes

The irises get angled slightly upwards when these people look

at someone, or smile. These eyes are very sensual and erotic. But don't confuse them with sleepy or drunk eyes, as these eyes are very rare, and are not heavy-lidded like sleepy, or drunk eyes. These eyes are only slightly angled upwards, and not a lot, so don't compare them to a squint, or any other eye disorder, or eye type. Formally, these eyes represent the eyes of Lord Shiva, the Supreme Yogi who is always in a trance. People with such eyes have unmatched knowledge, administrative, and political abilities. These people generally rule the hearts of others, wherever they are and people love them on deep emotional and sentimental levels. These people are certainly like Gods for the common masses. So, think thousands of times before hurting them. Even if you only have plans of hurting them, be careful, because once you have even tried to hurt them in any way, they don't need to react to anything, but their followers will show you their real emotions. Their followers love them madly and nothing could be more deadly, devastating, and destructive then their followers. Just keep in mind the picture of Lord Shiva, before trying to harm these people in any way. They certainly are very powerful and devastating and do not act or react very quickly but, people love them deeply and are associated with them sentimentally.

Albert Einstein had such eyes. These people are blessed with extraordinary mental calibre and certainly possess destructive powers, but don't use them unless absolutely necessary. However, once these people make up their minds to destroy someone, then only God could come in their way and save their target, otherwise the complete destruction of their targets is inevitable (remember Albert Einstein was instrumental in bringing destruction to Japan during the Second World War).

6. Uneven Eyes

In these eyes, both irises might be slightly uneven. If the irises

are uneven then these people possess the quality of judging, and seeing things, from two different angles. They can certainly see things which others cannot, and can judge any situation more aptly than a normal person. You cannot lie to them, or hide anything from them.

7. Elliptical Eyes

These eyes are elongated and the eyelids cover a large part of the iris. Those who are very enthusiastic and love speed and excitement have elliptical eyes. Most people who make sports their career, or who are interested in racecourses, race cars, or motorbikes have such eyes. They love speed. They might also be into martial arts and gymnastics as they are physically very active. These people also tend to be very diplomatic when it comes to relationships, whether it is business or personal. They generally speak their mind and like glorifying themselves in the public.

8. Wolf Eyes

As the name itself suggests, these eyes look dangerous and threatening. The wolf eyes are generally characterised by a small pupil with white irises or very light or faded irises. These people sometimes do not have an iris and only have a pupil in the middle of their eyes or irises, or their irises might be so small that it becomes difficult to find the difference between their irises and pupils. Such eyes indicate cruel and wicked natures, which are made obvious by the person's hard feelings for others.

9. Shallow or Deep-Set Eyes

Shallow eyes or deep-set eyes are those, which are set deep within the face, with jutting bones around the eyes.

People with shallow or deep-set eyes are very intense, loyal, compassionate, and hardworking. They have very keen observation skills and are quite idealistic. They are self-motivated and are inspired by life and things which they closely observe. Most writers and people in creative fields have such eyes. As these people are very hardworking and observe things keenly, so you will also find them doing well in the administrative field as well. They make capable administrators, as they are task-oriented and their judgments are sound. However, these people usually become successful after they reach their late thirties, if other good omens are not present on their face.

10. Doggy Eyes

People with such eyes look and behave very innocently and

because of this, they get help very easily. They also watch things very closely. They are very attracted towards the opposite sex and like to watch their partners undress, and are fierce lovers. These people are also very sexual in nature and the partner might take advantage of this attribute and dominate them in their personal lives.

11. Protruding Eyes

Protruding eyes project outwards from the eye socket, making what seems to be a convex curve. Some of them protrude outwards to an unnatural extent. These eyes are not counted in the beautiful eyes category. People with such eyes are often punished for someone else's faults. People with such eyes also possess certain temperaments with peculiar dispositions.

These people may also face a lot of emotional as well as mental difficulties in their life, especially in their youth. These eyes also indicate that problems will be caused by their family, peers, and associates. However, these people tend to become very successful during their middle age, especially during ages 35-40.

12. Wide Eyes

The eyes are wide open and the irises are clearly visible from all sides, in this eye type. In other eye categories, some part of the iris is covered by the eyelids, but for people with wide eyes, no part of their iris is covered by the eyelids, and the entire iris is clearly visible from all sides.

People with wide eyes possess a sharp intellect and have great memory powers. These eyes also indicate their excellent confidence. These people also have a good understanding about life and about their own profession, or domain. They can also explain things to others, with a totally different viewpoint making it easy for people to understand things quickly. These qualities make them suitable for taking up any profession in the field of academics. These people are also found in science and research-related subjects because of their good understanding, astuteness, sharp intellect and ability to look beyond things, which is generally difficult for people with normal understanding.

However, there are others in the wide eye category, who seem to have such wide open eyes, that it appears as if they have applied a lot of pressure on their eyes, but that is not the case. Vedic face readers are of the opinion that people with such eyes, possess violent natures, as it is generally observed that when a person is very angry then the eyes becomes very wide.

13. Sleepy Eyes

In these eyes the person's eyelids sit heavily over the eyes, and it seems that the person hasn't slept properly, but this is not the case. People with sleepy eyes are deeply sexual. So, men and women falling in this category have a libidinous nature. Women belonging to this category often turn out to be nymphomaniacs, if they also have thick or pouting lips.

People with such eyes have ill-fortunes. Their friends and colleagues might use them to fulfil their own purposes and betray them. They also might be belittled in front of people for useless reasons.

14. Droopy Eyes

Droopy eyes are those that bend or slant downwards. A little flabbiness can be observed below the eyes. These eyes convey weariness, despondency, dejection, and a morose spirit. These people are hardly interested in anything and are very lazy, casual, and non-committal. They are dejected spirits who generally see the negative side of everything.

15. Slanting Eyes

These are eyes that generally slant upwards. Such eyes have a different meaning for men and women. For men, these eyes are compared to those of the eagle, while for women these eyes are compared with those of the cat. For men, these eyes signify good vision and learning and they are generally scholars or masters in their subjects. People with such eyes generally become successful without lots of hardship. In women, these eyes bestow shrewdness, a lustful nature, and an opportunity-seeking attitude.

16. Downward Angled Eyes

Such eyes are in the mode of ignorance and will have all the features of people in the mode of ignorance. Such eyes indicate darkness, madness, anger, indolence, and sleep as well as blind consciousness. Such eyes portray anger and are generally not good for the person possessing them in any way, may it be

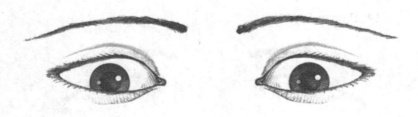

professionally, mentally, or spiritually. People generally get annoyed by listening to, or even looking at these people, because it seems as if they are tearing their eyelids, to unleash their anger upon the person they are looking at. These people might get addicted to intoxicants and waste their life on useless things.

17. Small or Scanty Eyes

These eyes are smaller than normal eyes and the person with such eyes possesses a beauty of exceptional quality. These people are very thoughtful, highly sophisticated, active, and agile. They always tend to be calm and analytical. Because of their calm behaviour, these people tend to make good friends and companions even with people who are rash and aggressive. Generally, fire signs have such eyes. Small-eyed people are generally, fastidious, hard-working, and specialise in a subject. They speak less and most of the people falling in this category are generally introverts.

EYE-SPACING

1. Widely Spaced Eyes

There needs to be more than one vertical eye gap between the left and the right eyes of a person, for their eyes to be included in this category. The more the gap between both the eyes, the more

widely spaced they are. Widely spaced eyes generally indicate that the person is indifferent about the effect of his/her behaviour. These people are generally not concerned about the world and their surroundings. They are generally very careless, more than any common person. They develop their own lifestyle and make judgments about everything, and are not concerned whether they are right or wrong. These people tend to be slow when it comes to making decisions and need lots of time and room to breathe. They tend to procrastinate and delay their work and schedules because of their slothful nature.

2. Very Closely Spaced Eyes

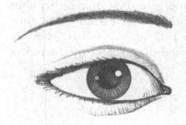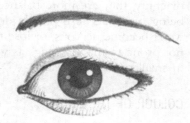

If the left and the right eyes do not have much gap between them and they seem to be almost sticking to each other, then these eyes are said to be closely spaced. These people have a narrow opinion and view of the world and have very little tolerance for people, especially if things do not tend to go their way. They are never completely satisfied with anything and always expect more from people and situations. Even in their personal life, it becomes hard for these people to tolerate external influences like temperature changes, traffic jams etc., which makes them lose their temper.

However, someone with closely spaced eyes also has a very strong ability to concentrate. When these people concentrate, they are very focused and hate being disturbed by someone, so they might get easily stressed. These people also tend to crack under pressure and need constant encouragement to work and develop their self-confidence.

3. Perfectly Spaced Eyes

As stated earlier, the most auspicious eyes are those which are neither very closely spaced, nor too widely spaced. People with perfectly spaced eyes possess balanced temperaments and judgements. While giving their opinion about a particular person or entity, they are more balanced and give their opinion without being biased. These people do not work in extremes, so they won't become nervous, or lose their patience very often. They are not prone to mood swings as well, and do not lose their tempers in small matters.

COLOUR OF THE EYES

The colour of the eyes is very important when determining the nature and characteristics of a person. The colour of the eyes also plays a significant role in determining the sexuality and behavioural pattern of people. The colour of the eyes reflects how strong, powerful, dominant, aggressive, or submissive a person generally is. The colour is basically determined by the colour of the irises. Let us discuss in detail the role each colour plays in judging the personality and character of an individual.

1. Dark Brown

Dark brown eyes represent the superiority of a person. People with dark brown eyes are generally individuals with strong characters and unflinching determination. Based on the hue, these eyes are counted among the most superior types of eyes.

Men with such eyes are very generous and warm (women are so only if they are well-balanced) and love their family and like to provide all the comforts to their family. These men are very committed in personal relationships, but their partners need to reciprocate and demonstrate their love and affection correctly with them. If the partners of such people are of the same intensity as they are, then they will have a very happy family life.

Dark brown eyes also represent the higher knowledge and intellect of a person. These people also work very hard and stretch themselves to their limit to satisfy their employers. However, they need appropriate rewards, from time to time, for the hard work they have put into their jobs. These people are very patient and can wait for a long time for rewards and promotions; however others should not take advantage of their nature, because if they do not receive the position of power and authority in their companies, they won't be able to survive for long in the company.

Even children with dark brown eyes have a good amount of ego combined with a playful and friendly nature. These children are very obedient but should not be abused or treated with disrespect if they tend to disobey sometimes. These children have their own thought processes, so it should be considered that because of this, they are working in their own way for better results.

2. Light Brown Eyes

These people are similar to those with dark brown eyes, however dark brown eyes represents a higher level of superiority, dominance, power and control than light brown eyes. People in both these categories are very serious and loyal towards their consorts, however people with dark brown eyes are more physically, mentally, and emotionally attached to their consorts and any kind of separation affects the people with dark brown eyes a lot on the physical, mental, and emotional levels. However, their light brown eyed counterparts have the ability to withdraw unscathed from unhappy and unsuccessful relationships.

Brown eyes (whether it is dark brown, or light brown) are not considered good for women in the Vedic context, as the features of this category refers to Shiva or the Yang principles, which represents dominance, aggression, and authority in relationships. This eye represents an outgoing nature as well. Dark brown eyes are generally referred to as the blazing sun, so this eye colour often bestows a fiery nature as well. Women with light brown eyes are better than their dark brown eye counterparts, as women with dark brown eyes tend to be more abrupt and blunt, because they function more emotionally than men. So the lighter the brown colour, the better the effect for women. For dark brown eyed men, the light brown eyed women are very compatible. These women tend to be more loyal, respecting, and obedient to the dark brown eyed men, than to any other category.

3. Deep Blue Eyes

If the irises of a person are deep blue in colour, it indicates that the person is highly sexual in nature. Women with deep blue eyes have a very fervent desire to look beautiful and sexy and to display their sexiness. These women become great assets in the professions of modelling, advertising, and films, where there is a need for lots of exposure. Both men and women with deep blue eyes feel a constant need for sex, for their physical, mental and emotional well-being. These people are also very caring and well-mannered.

4. Light Blue Eyes

The light blue-eyed counterparts are also highly sexed as their deep blue-eyed counterparts, however these people need more variety in sex and romantic relationships. These people are not as sentimental as their deep blue eyed counterparts and are more fun loving and outgoing. A light blue eyed woman's onscreen persona is more friendly and daring than the deep blue eyed ones, as the deep blue eyed ones are more shy. Being flirtatious in nature, these people are not as well-mannered as their deep blue-eyed counterparts, and are more wild, outspoken, and candid.

5. Grey Blue Eyes

This colour is very light and it is sometimes difficult to

determine the exact colour of the eye, however this is the lightest shade in the blue eye category. Sexually, these people have the same amount of passion as the deep blue eyed people, but these people are much more controlled in their behaviour than their two other counterparts.

6. Deep Green Eyes

Deep green eyed people reflect the same nature and traits as the light blue-eyed category. These people have the same amount of energy as the blue eyed ones, and like the light blue-eyed ones have the same amount of sexual appetite. The green eyed ones however are more talented and creative. Women falling in the deep green eye category use more of their imagination and creativity on camera, if they are in the glamour profession.

7. Light Green Eyes

People with light green eyes are more intellectual and practical in their approach and need an explanation for anything before they start on any endeavour. However, both the categories of green-eyed people could sometimes be very difficult to deal with, especially if the subject is a woman.

8. Black Eyes

Black-eyed individuals are very rarely seen in this world. Black signifies beauty. Black-eyed individuals are not as competent in worldly affairs as the other eye categories. Black-eyed people also tend to be very rigid in their ideologies, especially if they are women. Women who have such eyes are very difficult to convince and deal with, especially in the areas of sex and romance, because these women possess a narrow-mind and conservative outlook regarding these subjects. Black-eyed men are also not very competitive and remain content in their profession, without having much concern for worldly affairs.

9. Grey Eyes

Grey eyed people fall into the most dominant and conservative category. This feature will however be more dominant, depending upon the racial groups the person belongs to.

10. Hazel Eyes

Hazel eyes represent a galaxy of phenomena. Firstly, these people fall into one of the categories of brown eyes, but the colour is more like red wine. However, unlike the dark brown eyed individuals, these people will either have a more dominant physical side, or a more dominant mental side, but these people cannot be both at the same time. These people also possess very convivial natures, with a good sense of humour and often possess a lot of warmth in personal relationships. However, they are not as attached to the family as the dark brown eyed people. These people believe in accumulating various items of luxury in their home, as they wish to live a luxurious life. In case of women, the same rule applies, as is applied to those with brown eyes as per Vedic illustrations. The magnitude of worldly desire in these people is far more, so women in these categories tend to choose their career over relationships, and will not like or tolerate restrictions of any kind.

SOME OTHER CHARACTERISTICS OF THE EYES AND THEIR SIGNIFICANCE

Let us discuss in detail different signs and marks present in the eyes and their effect upon the personality, nature, character, and destiny of a person.

(1) *Red lines present on the sides of the eyes*: If a couple of red lines, or a red vein in visible in the sides of the eyes, it indicates that the person is very hardworking and is task-oriented. If the other features of the face are good, they easily gain a position of power and authority. One of the predictions usually made for people with red edges, or red ends in the eyes, is that they become great emperors.

(2) *White and crystal clear eyes*: If the eyes are totally white and crystal clear, it indicates that the person possesses an easygoing and stress free nature and has good health and vitality.

(3) *Reddish Eyes*: If the whole eye becomes red sometimes then this indicates some eye related problems; especially irritation, and stress as well as lack of sleep. However if the whole eye is permanently red and too many red veins appear on the eyes then

it indicates a really bad temper.

(4) *Black or blue lines*: People with black or blue lines inside the eyes on either side of the cornea indicate serious and complicated health problems, basically related to the liver or kidney.

(5) *Yellow lines*: Yellow lines also indicate health hazards like the blue ones. These lines are usually present in people who suffer from diseases like typhoid, cholera, extreme physical weakness, or mental anxiety and madness. Permanently yellow eyes indicate that the liver of the person is damaged.

(6) *White spots visible around the irises*: If white spots are visible on any side of the iris, it is an indication of serious accidents. People with permanent white spots upon the iris, suffer from health hazards.

(7) *White spots visible below the iris*: White spots, or marks, on the lower part of the iris indicate a sharp contrast in the person's motives and actions. These people are in constant clash with the world, as well as their own people. There are chances that these people might not be on good terms with their children, brothers, and family.

(8) *Shifty eyes:* Shifty eyes indicate shyness and lack of confidence. Sometimes shyness is linked with selfishness in Vedic contexts. Blinking a lot is often a symptom of mental instability.

(9) *Large pupils:* Eyes with large pupils indicate that the absorption capacity of light is more in the eyes. The sun is usually dominant in their astrological chart. These people attain glory and power at a very early stage in their life because of the dominant influence of the Sun which is a strong indicator of glory, power, and money. However, people with large pupils often tend to have weak eyesight.

(10) *Small pupils:* People with small pupils are most often reserved and calculated in their behaviour, and do not attain the level of glory and power as those with large pupils. This is because they are shy, hesitant, and afraid of taking risks.

(11) *Large eyes with small pupils:* Large eyes often indicate an outgoing and friendly nature, however if these eyes have small pupils, then these people are hesitant and shy and are introverts.

(12) *Shiny eyes:* People whose eyes are bright and shiny with a sparkle represent an evolved spiritual consciousness. Indian transcendentalists are of the opinion that shiny eyes possess a mystical vision and are often possessed by people who have powerful and strong magnetic personalities. These eyes are very hypnotic and the masses are very often persuaded by whatever these people say or do, and tend to follow the paths set by them. If the other facial features and omens are good, then these people possess unmatched calibre and spiritual vision.

CHAPTER 8

EARS

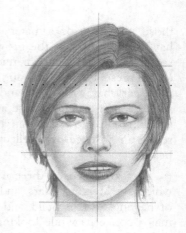

Ears are the best indicators of a person's childhood inclinations, ideologies, and dreams, because the ears determine one's fortune from birth till the age of 14, and are the best way of finding out the person's nature, inclination, abilities, and possibilities. The ears have a profound impact upon one's life and understanding it can help the reader find the deep inner secrets of a person. A large part of the person's ability, worth, nature, characteristics, and destiny are very easily revealed by studying the ears.

The shape of the ears resemble the foetus in the womb of the mother and the Vedic scriptures are of the opinion that the overall shape, size, colour and position of the ears will reveal how the baby was nourished and treated in the early years of the nursing period during childhood.

The left ear generally indicates the life of a person from birth till seven years and the right ear indicates life from 8-14 years. The overall shape of the ears does not change as the child grows from infancy to adulthood, so the basic shape of the ears remains the same, however only the size increases. It might sound astonishing, but it is a fact that the ears are the only parts of the body that tend to grow throughout life. So, the older the person gets, the larger the ears become; especially if the person works on an intellectual plane. It is revealed in the Vedic scriptures that people who work on an intellectual plane have ears that grow faster than those who work on a material plane. Materialistic people tend to have smaller ears as the growth of their ears tends to stagnate sometime in the youth or middle age. Large and well-developed ears represent good luck during a person's childhood. Large and thick earlobes with good and fleshy inner and outer helixes are also the sign of intelligence and are often associated with wealth and long life. However, thin and poorly shaped outer helixes may reveal an absence of intellect and wealth, as well as diminished health.

Ears are ruled by three major planets in Vedic physiognomy which are Mercury, Mars, and Saturn. Saturn also rules the sense of hearing. So size, build, and placement of the ears should be the major concerns while looking at the ears because these are the main factors in determining the foundation of life and a person's potential. Now, let us discuss the significance of different shapes, sizes, positions, and features of the ears in detail.

POSITION OF THE EARS

1. Tip of Ears Higher than the Eyebrows

If the tip of the ears is higher than the corners of the eyebrows then the person works on an intellectual plane. These people possess great intellect and are generally interested in arts, philosophy, writing, and research. These people also possess a very unique quality of receiving information faster than others. Their recollection is also superior as compared to others. Most people whose ear tips are set higher than their eyebrows attain name, fame, and wealth at an early age, by the time they are 28.

2. Tip of Ears Reaching the Eyebrows

If the tips of the ears sit in line with the eyebrows, i.e. they do not reach above the eyebrows, it indicates that the person is metaphysical, but is still interested in the physical side of the world. The difference between these people and people of the previous category is that those in the previous categories (i.e. people whose ear tips are higher than the corners of the eyebrows) have high intuitive powers and

these people have a higher general ability. People in this category generally achieve success in their midlife. The age group 28-40 is generally considered good for these people since that is when they reach the peak of their careers.

3. Ears Distinctly lower than the Eyebrows

These people are hardcore materialists and avid pleasure seekers. Ears that are lower than the eyebrows also indicate a struggle in the early years, especially during childhood and teens. These people are very much attracted towards the bodily conception of life. Their sexual orientation is more dominant than their other interests in life. Since most of them have had a turbulent childhood, that's the reason why as adults, they grow up hankering for enjoyments, comfort, and material pleasures. Women in this

category tend to use their bodies to the fullest to get what they desire, and men will work ruthlessly and impatiently to fulfil their physical needs. Their processing of information is very slow. Any information or instruction given to them should be fed very slowly and should be aided with proper diagrams, pictures, and visuals at every possible step, to make them understand things easily and accurately. These people generally achieve success much later in life and if other auspicious marks are not present upon their face then the level of their success is very mediocre. Some of these people might achieve success at an early age, if other signs on their face are good.

4. Upper Portion of Ears Sticking out Horizontally

When the upper portions of the ears stick out horizontally to a great extent, this indicates a childhood which was filled with extremes. In some cases people might have lost their parents quite early, or they might not have been very close to their parents. In other cases, these people might have got so much attention as children from their parents, or other family members (this is indicated by ears in which the outer edge of the ears are puffy) that they might have become very selfish as adults. In both cases, these ears indicate that these people did not have an ideal childhood. Most of these people are not close to their parents. They also do not give too much importance to the needs of their spouses and are always keen to fulfil their own needs and desires.

5. Upper Portion of Ears Pressed inside Horizontally

This category of people are quite unlike the above category of people. As in the previous case in which the upper portion of the ears sticks out horizontally, it represents that the person concerned is quite detached from family and is not emotionally close to family members, likewise when the upper portion of the ears is pressed inside horizontally, it indicates that the individual is very much attached and close to his family. The people in this category are only concerned with their home and family.

6. Upper Portion of the Ears Angled Back Vertically

If the upper portions of the ears are slightly angled back vertically, then these people are generally tough people to deal with. Their opinions are generally formed and based upon their own faiths and beliefs, which they generally form through beliefs that are aligned with what they have practically seen, or observed. These people have their own set of rules and regulations and are very unconventional in the way they choose to do things. They are also very stubborn and adamant.

7. Upper Portion of the Ears Totally Parallel to lower Portion

These people fall in the category of people who like to choose the middle path. They might have some set of rules and

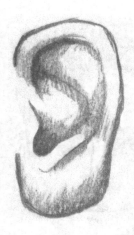

regulations, but do not believe in rigid observations. These people are concerned only with the facts, without looking at how subtle one has to be. They are also very good at following instructions, and hence make good disciples, especially if they have long ears and earlobes.

8. Upper Portion of the Ears Angled or Pressed Forward

If the upper portions of the ears are angled forward or even if the back of the upper portion of the ear is pressed then this generally indicates that the person has low confidence levels. Because of lack of perseverance and will-power, these people are not able to stick with their undertaken tasks and tend to break their promises quickly. If the back of the upper portion of the ears is pressed, or deformed, then the person may be a pessimist, who does not have any interest in learning either through their own endeavours, or even under the guidance of someone else. These people tend to look at the negative aspects of everything and may neither be learned, nor cultured, if they have not had a good background.

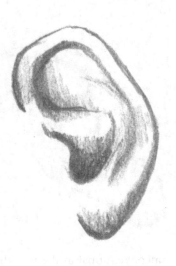

EAR SIZES

1. Medium Ears

These ears are neither too big nor too small, but are of medium shape, size, and placement. These ears can be included in the ideal ear category, if other aspects of these ears are good. If

the tip of these ears is above
the corners of the eyebrows,
or in line with the corners of
the eyebrows, then these ears
are considered to have
auspicious qualities. However,
if the tips of these ears are
lower than the eyebrows, then
these ears are not so
auspicious. People who belong
to this category are very
balanced in their life,
behaviour, and outlook. They
are neither too detached from
material pleasures, nor are too
attached, when it comes to
acquiring material amenities, or

pleasures in life. They neither work on an extremely intellectual, or
spiritual plane, nor on a gross material, or sensual plane, but
possess an even outlook. A medium ear length also indicates that
these people are very flexible in the listening departments and
outlook as well.

2. Large Ears

Big or large ears are fully
grown, well developed with
large or fully developed ear
lobes as well. If the tip of
these ears is above the
eyebrows, then these people
tend to work on a deep
intellectual and spiritual plane.
If the tip of these ears are not
above the eyebrows, but reach
the corners of the eyebrows,
then these people work on a
material plane, with regard to
spiritual activities. However, if
the tip of these ears is lower

than the eyebrows, then these people work only on a gross material plane. In all the above mentioned cases, these ears are pure signals of a person's vitality and independence. Long ears also signify an exceptional listening ability. These people generally soak up information the way a dry sponge absorbs water. If these people work on an intellectual plane, there are chances that these people might become great philosophers, scientists, philanthropists, writers, or artists.

3. Small Ears

Small and chunky ears indicate a person's interest in the gross physical, or material side of the world. These ears are generally not considered good for processing and storing a lot of information in the brain. These ears have the capacity to grab only a piece of information at a time. If lots of complex information is given to them quickly, they will try to juggle everything and will get confused and forget everything. However the position of these ears should be clearly seen and identified. Very often these ears are positioned much below the eyebrows and the eyes as well. However, very rarely the tip of these ears is found reaching the eyebrows. In both these cases, the results will be different. Let us discuss both these cases in detail:

(1) Small ears positioned below the eyebrows: People with small ears that are positioned below the outer corners of the eyebrows are gross sensualists. Small ears also indicate a person's low tolerance level when it comes to tolerating people and things which are not as per their expectations. The lower the ears are placed (below the eyebrows), the less tolerant the person is.

(2) Small ears with the upper portion above the eyebrow corners: Small ears, whose upper portions are above the eyebrows,

indicate the amalgamation of physical and metaphysical attitudes and behaviours. These people tend to dislike dullness and moroseness a lot, because a morose environment takes away their energy and life. These people should have a healthy and satisfied personal and professional life, and their sex life should remain very active if they are to be physically and mentally sound.

EAR SHAPES

1. Triangular Ears

These ears and earlobes are not very fleshy and generally show a triangular upward curve. These ears are not good for success and achievement, and represent an enraged personality. These people tend not to be happy from within, because of their family conditions, or an unhappy childhood. So these people tend to grow into very irresponsible adults. They might also be very rash and violent, and might adopt a revengeful nature.

2. Squarish or Rectangular Ears

Squarish or rectangular ears are indicative of selfish and shrewd behaviour. These people tend to be more cunning when their ears are without any earlobes or when they have a very small and negligible lobe. If other features of their faces are not good, then these people could also be devoid of good friends and colleagues and might have to spend a solitary life. The latter part of their lives is especially not so happy because they have no company around them. Their old age might be full of emotional

and psychological difficulties because of this.

3. Elf-Shaped Ears

Elf-Shaped Ears   Side view of Elf-Shaped Ears

If the upper parts of the ears are pointed then it is called elf-shaped. It looks as if there is a bone jutting out from the upper part of their ears. These people are often very capricious and very rebellious. They are very moody and do things as per their own desire and mood. These people also tend to have a sharp intellect and are very creative and independent. They need a lot of space at work as well as in relationships to adjust and perform. However, these people are also very outgoing and friendly. They also have a good sense of humour, so they entertain their friends and colleagues a lot. These people are very broad minded and modern in their approach and outlook. Narrow-minded and conservative attitudes, or behaviour turns them off.

4. Round and Big Ear Tips

People with big and rounded ear tips are curious. These people understand everything very easily and are exceptionally smart and dexterous. They use their intellect and energies only for things they are deeply interested in and do not believe in wasting their energy and intellectual resources on things that are not fertile. They are also very dedicated and hardworking. You will find several workaholics in this category. They should endeavour to find their own niche and strengths to excel in their life.

5. Ears with Puffy Outer Edges

If the outer edges of the ears are puffy then these people tend to be

Side view

irresponsi-ble. They tend to be very selfish and disregard the other person's feelings and emotions. They wish to get the most out of people and situations and tend to be very mean when it comes to fulfilling their desires.

6. Ears with an extremely thin outer edge

Ears with an extremely thin outer edge indicate the lack of vitality within a person. These people lack self-

confidence and when they are not able to achieve success, they very shrewdly put the fault of their failure on others. They also lack the desire to persevere and put in hard work, and use others to fulfil their motives and desires.

7. Protruding Ears

Protruding ears are those which stick out in an irregular fashion. These people tend to be very lonely in their lives. In their childhood, they might have been separated from their parents, since they were unwanted or due to other reasons. Either their parents have put them in a boarding school, or they might not have been very close to their parents. These people have a very original way of thinking and are quite creative. They are also very energetic and physical. They also do well in sports that are very strenuous and tiring.

8. Extremely Minute and Miniature Ears

These ears are unlucky in terms of the overall growth and development of a person. These people are deprived of the basic amenities of life. However, these people are very close to their parents, siblings, and friends and tend to get lots of love, and affection during their childhood.

9. Deformed Ears

Ears which do not have a proper shape and size and are deformed in some way are highly inauspicious. These people tend to have a very deformed life as they lack reason. They are generally prone to receiving a hard blow from fate. These people will work in the most abominable conditions, if their natal charts do not have other good signs. They do not have a very long life. Most of them also face punishments meted out by law and nature. These people might also be wicked.

10. Hairy Ears

Ears with a thick growth of hair are certainly a good sign in terms of health and vitality. This means that these people possess a very good healthy, long life. They are very arrogant and tend to get angry quickly; however, their anger is short-lived. These people also need to control their expenses because they tend to spend more than what is required. If the growth of hair on the ears is heavy, and not proportionate to the hair on the body, then these people waste their talents, energy and money on futile things.

11. Ears with Large Holes

Holes are generally the doors or the gateways of reception. People who have large ear holes are very good listeners, as compared to others. They possess an equilibrium of thoughts and reasoning and have a willingness to learn things from others.

12. Ears with Small Holes

People who possess small ear holes are less receptive and lack concentration. These people generally do not understand everything very easily and need an elaborate explanation. They also tend to be rigid in their ideas and behaviour and are not receptive to new concepts. These people are also very narrow-minded. Small ears with small holes represent lack of confidence and these people tend to get scared and panic even in minor situations. Don't expect a lot of help from these people, as they are not very big-hearted.

EARLOBES

Earlobes are the lower fleshy portion of the ears. Earlobes play an important part in face reading. Let's discuss the significance of different types of earlobes.

TYPES OF EARLOBES

1. Long Earlobes

This is the category Buddha belonged to. Long earlobes are those which hang very low towards the neck, making your ears look very long. Long earlobes are indicators of a long and healthy life. These earlobes also indicate that the person is gifted with a unique sense of understanding and judgment. These people decipher reckoning powers. Nothing in front of their eyes goes unnoticed. These earlobes also represent good luck, in terms of material as well as spiritual success. Everything tends to flow towards these people very easily. They are also very independent, strong minded, and intellectual.

2. Medium Earlobes

Medium earlobes are often small, and most people have such ears. These people are very stoic, dexterous, active, and agile. They are very observant, and possess unique observation powers. They are also great inventors and have a great flair for creativity. You will find most filmmakers, writers, and scientists all over the world have medium earlobes. These people live a life with depth and meaning.

3. Very Small Earlobes

Very small earlobes are not considered to be very lucky. These people waste their energies and skills on useless things and lack creation and initiative. They are generally promiscuous and do not achieve sexual fulfilment easily. As these people are not very hardworking, so they generally adopt sleazy methods for easy cash flow.

4. Narrow Earlobes

Narrow earlobes are generally thin and less in diameter as compared to normal earlobes. People with narrow earlobes are impulsive and lack patience. They are also prone to unnecessary mood swings and are not very trustworthy. These ears are not good for success as they lack determination. People with narrow earlobes are said to have broken lives as they tend to lose their wealth and relationships because of their impulsiveness.

5. Thick Earlobes

People with thick earlobes have a large group of friends. They also work and strive hard in their careers and their wealth generally keeps on increasing, as thick earlobes are very good indicators of surplus wealth. Women with thick earlobes, especially ones with long earlobes, are very lucky for their husbands as they bring a lot of wealth for their husbands.

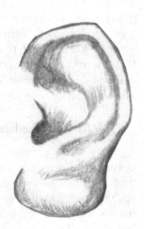

6. No Earlobes

Those ears, which are completely joined from top to bottom, have no room for the earlobes. People who do not have earlobes are not very lucky. These people do not have a clear cut vision of what they want in their life. Their minds are always wavering and fluctua-ting. If other marks on their faces indicate good fortune, then these people will have to struggle with different careers before they finally settle down in one career. These people are also hardcore materialists and gross sensualists, as well as selfish and shrewd.

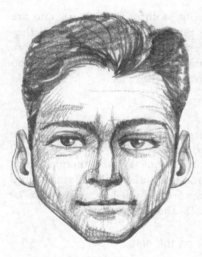

No Earlobe   Side view

EAR COLOUR

The colour of the ears is very important, as this plays an important role in determining and judging the temperament of a person. It is also a vital source of life energy. If the colour of the ears are good and properly matches the hue of the person's skin on the rest of the body, then the ears are generally considered to be good. Now, let us discuss in detail the effect of different colours on the life and destiny of a person.

1. Ears lighter in colour and tone than the face

Ears that are slightly lighter in tone than the colour of the face are considered to be highly auspicious. Lighter toned ears generally indicate a famous reputation. If these people are into the show business, they will have a huge breakthrough. However, if other marks of their faces are not good, then these people might also have a very notorious reputation or might be defamed. They might also become famous for unwanted reasons.

2. Ears darker in colour and tone than the face

People who possess darker ear tones very often lack life's vital energies. These people are prone to slothful behaviours, and are not very hardworking. They also possess sensual natures, so they very often waste their time and energies on sensual gratification. These people also lack concentration, as ears darker than the skin tone of the face represent gloom and ignorance.

3. Red ears

If the colour of the ear is permanently red, then it is a strong indication of lust. People with red ears are often very lusty as well as vain, arrogant, and egoistic. These people are also inconsiderate, ungrateful, and not benevolent. They also lack stamina and will-power and most often suffer from high blood pressure or some other dangerous or incurable disease.

4. Permanent red veins visible on the ears

If red veins appear on the ears then this person has a really bad temper. This person possesses a fanatic disposition and has the tendency to go out of control anytime.

CHAPTER 9

NOSE

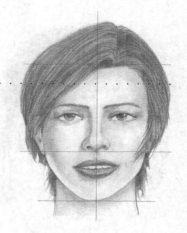

The nose is ruled by the planet Mars according to Vedic physiognomy and is generally represented as the Third House of Wealth in face reading. The nose is also an important indicator of the character and nature of a person, for which the clefts and bridge of the nose are studied. In Vedic face reading, the nose also helps us determine how much sexual drive, leadership qualities, power, ego, empathy and warmth a person has. The nose also plays an important role in determining the quality of one's mid-life (40-50).

In Vedic face reading, several categories of noses are mentioned. Now, let us discuss each and every feature of the nose in detail.

CATEGORISATION OF THE NOSE ACCORDING TO ITS LENGTH

1. Long Nose

In Vedic physiognomy, it is clearly defined how to determine long, short, and mediocre noses. First, horizontally divide your face into three sections as illustrated at the start of this book regarding the division of the face. If the middle section is the longest, then the person belongs to the category of those with a long nose. Long nosed people are those who fall into the mode of passion. As described earlier, people in the mode of passion are materialistic. People with long noses generally need a job which is

very comfortable and which gives them a lot of money and authority. You will rarely find these people willing to work as sweepers, cleaners, receptionists etc. These people have a lot of ego and attitude and hate to receive orders.

2. Middle/Moderate Length Nose

This is the ideal length among all nose types (according to length) as this nose is neither too long, nor too short. If you divide the face into three sections, the middle section of the nose will be more or less equal to the upper or the lower sections of the face. These noses are generally a boon if we consider the understanding and dexterity of a person in relation to his environment and work. People with such a nose are industrious, able, apt, dexterous, quick, witty, very active, and agile. This nose length is considered to have strong leadership vibrations, especially if the front part of the nose is round and pointed. These people have lots of patience and will-power and

they are skilful enough to use their brains with their brawns for greater achievements, without getting disturbed by external factors.

3. Short Nose

These noses are very easily identified, as the name itself suggests, these noses are very short in length and are very close to the eyes. If you horizontally divide the face into three sections, then the middle section will be the shortest in this category. People with this nose type have poor memories. They need a lot of time to learn and understand things. These people also lack interest in most things and are very disinterested in any project given to them. They are also prone to wasting their time in futile matters and certainly possess the 'passing the buck' attitude. These people also lack reasoning and are very poor in identifying beneficial situations and opportunities. They have laidback attitudes and are not good in any kind of intellectual field. However, if some pious marks are present on their face, then they can excel in sports, or those fields which require physical labour.

People with too short noses that are very close to the eyes are very timid as well. These people are low in their confidence and will-power. Children with such noses lack self-confidence and need constant reassurance and encouragement.

CATEGORISATION OF THE NOSE ACCORDING TO ITS WIDTH

1. Wide or Big Nose

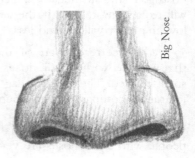

Big Nose

These noses are generally round and puffy and bigger in size than normal. There are generally two kinds of big noses.

a. Wide/Big Nose with Flat Head: If the front part of the nose, i.e. the head or tip of the nose is flat, it is not a good indicator of wealth in early life. People with such noses generally belong to the category of followers, as they lack will-power. These people generally live a mediocre life when they are young. Their financial condition generally becomes better during their middle age (40-50). These people are also very indecisive. They generally take a decision even though they are not perfectly sure, and then they regret it.

Big Nose with
Pointed Head

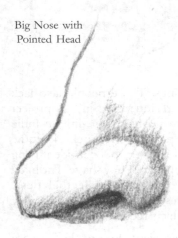

b. Wide/Big Nose with Pointed Head: Bigger noses that are pointed are considered to be very auspicious, and lucky. These noses are generally good indicators of wealth and fortune. These people generally live a good life in terms of money and riches. Even if these people are not born in rich families, they tend to get jobs at higher ranks (unless something is wrong in their natal charts). As the nose generally rules the age from 41-50, these people will have excellent fortune and luck during these years.

2. Small Nose

As the core work of the nose is to supply oxygen to the body, people with small noses generally inhale less oxygen as compared to people with large noses because people with small noses will have smaller nostrils, while people with bigger noses have larger nostrils. If the air intake is large, the heart will expand more, and if the air intake is low, the heart will expand less.

Vedic face readers are of the opinion that people with small noses are very small-hearted. These people lag behind in tolerance, compassion, and benevolence, while people with larger noses are more benevolent, and compassionate. Again, people with small noses are very shy and

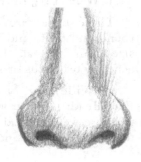

introverted and because of this, and their faint-heartedness, they do not think big, as people with bigger noses do. So, people having smaller noses will generally struggle throughout their lives to become successful (unless they are associated with someone powerful), as they do not take risks or make decisions easily. However, people with a small nose-width are more attentive, attractive, and detail-oriented, that's the reason you will find most of the airhostesses, flight stewards, bartenders, waiters, and secretaries have such a nose.

3. Ideal Nose

Ideal noses are neither too big, nor too small in their width. People with ideal noses are determined, savvy, and concerned about each and every aspect of their lives. They are also very artistic, aesthetic, and creative. This makes them perfectly fit for the profession of fine arts, theatre, television, acting, commercials, and films. Most actors, filmmakers, and celebrities around the world possess moderate width noses which are neither too broad, nor too narrow.

CATEGORISATION OF THE NOSE ACCORDING TO ITS HEIGHT

The height of the nose is determined by the tip of the nose. If the height of the nose is good, the tip of the nose will be elevated; whereas if the height is less the nose tip will be flat. Now as per the height of the nose, there are two divisions:

1. Flat Nose

Noses that are flat basically lack edge and mount. These noses are low-set noses, if we measure the height of the tip of the nose from its base, i.e. from the philtrum. As these noses lack edge and mount, people with such noses lack direction in their life. These

people are generally not goal-oriented and are like straws blowing in the wind. They also lack initiative, so they want others to take the first step. They lack the qualities that are required for leadership.

2. Vertical Nose

Vertical noses are those that are well mounted giving a proper vertical shape to the nose. These are high-set noses that have higher nose bridges and higher nose tips, if we measure them from the base of the nose, or the philtrum. Normally vertical noses are very lucky if they are straight and are not angled towards the left or the right side of the face. As the vertical shape of the nose gives height and mount to the nose, people with these nose shapes are generally more reliable, determined, firm, resolute, and unshakable, like mountains. These people generally have more drive and ambition and are very focused. This nose indicates strong leadership qualities, abundant energy, pride, and a desire for change.

DIFFERENT TYPES OF NOSES

1. Eagle Nose/Hooked Nose

Eagle or hooked noses look like the hooked beak of an eagle. The nose ridge is high and the nose tip is sharply pointed downwards. The nostrils are also sometimes very exposed. These people possess very domineering and bossy natures. They hate to be dominated by others and hate to follow instructions. They just like to be dominating, whatever it might take. These people are also very demanding and uncompromising. They are also extremely self-centred and believe in exploiting and taking advantage of others. They also have a big sexual appetite. An aquiline nose also portrays a strong will. These people are very independent and enterprising and generally this talent develops and guarantees them success especially during mid-life. However, their financial condition will not be good during the initial years. These people are also very stingy and thrifty with money, so they will rarely be considerate about their family and children in terms of money. They are also very sceptical.

2. Pig Nose

The pig nose is not straight and is generally upturned, giving a convex shape to the nose. The easiest way to identify this correctly is to see the nose from the side; the horizontal line at the bottom of the nose is not horizontal, and is turned upwards. Generally, people with such noses are very lucky in terms of finances and become successful in their early adulthood or sometimes in their teens as well. If these people take part in

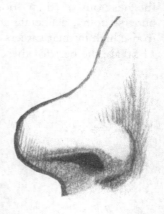

any pageants, or contests, they generally win them because of their sheer luck, even if they are not up to the mark. These people are very abrasive and candid in the way they talk, and because of this they might have to face a lot of problems in their professional lives, as people generally get easily offended by their behaviour. These people do not like to listen to anyone's advice or take orders from others. They like to work according to their rules. Women with such a nose are like free birds who like being independent. These women love money rather than their spouses, so this nose causes early break-ups in relationships and most often delays their marriage. Children with such noses are very naughty and sporty.

3. Swan Nose

The nose profile neither seems to be turned up, nor points downwards, but is straight like the swan's beak. People with such a nose are good natured and this nose is also called the 'gentleman's nose'. People with such noses do not believe in mudslinging, and do not uselessly get involved in back-biting, or pulling someone down. These people are generally good-hearted and believe in clean and hassle-free work. These noses are the best for business and entrepreneurial ventures, as these people tend to get the best out of their money and employees because of their understanding, deliberate actions, and wisdom. These people tend to rise high in their careers between the ages 28-35. The age group 41-50 are the best for these people in terms of luck and cash flow.

4. Lion Nose/Bulbous Nose

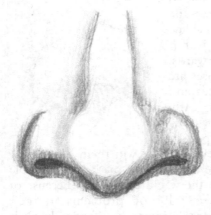

The Lion nose is also called the bulbous nose as this nose has a bulbous tip like that of a lion. Such a nose is also thick from both sides, i.e. the wings (the flesh) covering the nostrils is large and rounded. The three rounded sections are indications of a person's good luck in terms of money. Their luck and positive vibrations for money will increase during their middle years, especially between the ages 41-50. These people will also have good luck in gambling, especially if they buy lottery tickets, or invest in the share market. For women this nose does not produce good vibrations. These women will not have very good luck in terms of personal relationships, and marriage. This nose also indicates that the woman will have a lot of expenditures.

These women should also try and get married to a person who is much older than them, probably 10-15 years older, who could generally guide them in their life, as these women lack maturity.

5. Straight Nose

Straight noses are those that do not have any bumps on the bridge of the nose and the nose goes straight down without any indentations. People with straight noses are generally independent, broadminded, liberal, and free thinkers. These people are very straightforward, honest, and truthful. These people are also very hardworking, disciplined, steady, methodical, and decisive in their approach. Whatever might be the result of their actions; they always endeavour to get better results in their life and are never disappointed with negative results. As these people are very hardworking, steady, and determined, they usually reach the peak of their careers at a certain point in their life. Some of these people generally reach the peak as early as at the age of 35, if other omens on their faces are good. These people become successful businessmen, as this nose brings good vibrations for business and wealth. The ages 41-50 are very good in terms of luck.

6. Nose with Ridge on the Bridge

This nose does not have a totally straight bridge, but there will be a slight edge or elevation in the bridge of the nose. People with such a nose have a high IQ level. But, they are very rigid, proud, and stubborn. They generally work as per their own wishes and are not very close to their parents. Again,

as these noses have a ridge on the bridge; it generally works as a bump on the smooth road of their life's journey. These people will have a lot of ups and downs in their lives and will not have a smooth life. These people are also prone to mood swings, and sometimes tend to be very indecisive as well.

7. Curved Nose

The bridge of the nose is not straight but is a half-rounded curve from top to bottom. People with curved noses are very talented and are good forecasters of businesses. These people have great business acumen and are very successful. If they are in the business of filmmaking, they will have a lot of talent and are very lucky. These noses give the owner a powerful drive, ambition, and lots of energy. These people are generally untiring. However, it should be noted that these noses should not have any elevations or ridges on the bridge of the nose, otherwise the luck will change and the qualities of the ridged nose will be applicable for these people.

8. Nose with Round Tip

Round tips generally represent a curious personality. These people are generally very curious about everything. So if you tell them only one facet of a story and leave the rest, they will remain disturbed till they get the full information.

9. Heavy Nose/Nose with Large Round Tip

If the nose has a heavy, large, round tip, it indicates that the person is foolish. If children have such a nose, they are mostly poor in studies. These people have very low concentration levels.

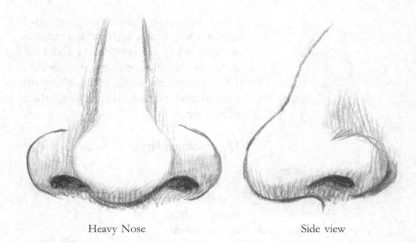

Heavy Nose   Side view

Clowns in the circus put on such noses during their act to make people laugh. Maybe subconsciously the clowns know that this nose type is related to stupidity in some way. This is not a very lucky nose in terms of success and wealth.

10. Elongated Nose

Elongated noses indicate lack of judgement. There is an unnatural distance between the tip and base of the nose. These people tend to portray the same stupidity and foolishness such as those who have a large round tipped nose. This nose might be sometimes lucky in terms of finances, if other features of the face are good and if these noses are shaped like the pig nose. It should be noted that long noses, in any case, indicate that the person is highly materialistic, and voluptuous.

11. Unbalanced Nose

These people have low tolerance levels and are impulsive.

They generally hate criticism and might turn violent for the smallest reasons. They do not have good luck in terms of relationships and wealth. They definitely need to work upon their attitude and need to change their behaviour a lot.

12. Deformed Nose

If the nose shape is deformed since birth, or becomes deformed due to some reason, then the person will face a lot of crisis in life. These people will lack all the basic facilities in life and will have to slog through their lives. They generally live a vile, mean, and wicked life.

13. Narrow, Sharp and Pointed Nose

Pointed noses indicate leadership qualities, high ideals, and a sharp memory. These people will also be mega-experts in their fields, curious about the smallest details and esoterically interested in their chosen fields. We can say that these people are very passionate about their work, or business, and have high business ethics, or standards. These people also dislike spending money frivolously and frequently. Most of these people are affluent and highly successful in business.

14. Thin and Bony Nose/Tortoise Nose

The bridge of the nose as well as the central section of the nose is extremely thin, bony, and small. These people are extremely self-centred. They will only think of taking from others. However, when it comes to giving, these people feel withdrawn, the same way the tortoise withdraws its limbs from all sides. These people are also deeply scared and bothered about everything. The outer world bothers them a lot. Also these people will not have a lot of friends, or will have no friends at all, and will always live a solitary life, like that of a tortoise.

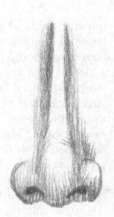

DIFFERENT FEATURES OF THE NOSE

The nose is a very important part of the face and helps in determining two major things, i.e. character and finances. This is one of the important sections that will make a person more apt in assessing the character of people, just by looking at the nose. Let's discuss the important features of the face, as per Vedic face reading.

1. Cleft on the Tip of the Nose

Vedic physiognomy is strongly of the opinion that a cleft on the tip of the nose represents the wicked, mean, and base nature of a person. The cleft can be either vertical on the tip of the nose, or horizontal on the sides of the tip of the nose. Horizontal clefts are seen on the sides of the tip, while the vertical cleft is seen at the middle of the tip. These are called the three bumps on the nose. A person may not have all the three dents, but any one of the dents on the nose will indicate the same thing as mentioned here. These

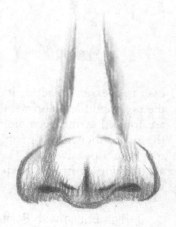

people possess extremely selfish natures and are grossly engaged in satisfying their yearning, desires, and appetites in a roguish way. People with clefts on their noses are always very dishonest and unprincipled. Their words, deeds, and mannerisms cannot be believed. They are only concerned about the fulfilment of their own cravings and yearnings. One more characteristic of noses with a cleft is that these people have some sexual perversions. Most women involved in the pornography industry and such professions have a cleft on their nose (i.e. horizontal or vertical clefts on the tip of the nose). These noses are not at all considered good in one's spouse. These noses also represent early family difficulties and obstruction in the flow of finances during the earlier years, especially during childhood and the teens. These people hanker for various objects of luxury and want those objects at any cost. These people also need to be cautious when they are in the age group 41-50, as they might see a lot of disruptions in personal and professional relationships during this period.

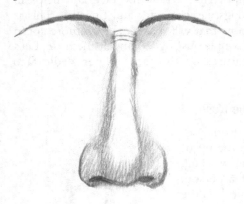

2. Horizontal Fold/Line at the Beginning of the Nose Bridge

If a person has one or two permanent horizontal lines (folds) at the beginning of the nose bridge, then the person is tough. These people are very demanding and are not very easy to please. However, if while contracting the nose and the eyebrows, three or more lines are formed at the beginning of the bridge of the nose, then these people are strong and tough, in a positive way. These people possess an undying spirit and keep on moving even under difficulties and negative circumstances.

3. High Bridge with Pointed Nose Tip

If the bridge of the nose is high and the person also has a pointed nose tip, then this is a good indication of wisdom as well as of power and authority. A high nose bridge indicates a high degree of energy, and a curious mind, whereas a pointed nose tip indicates the will for power and authority.

4. Visible Nostrils

People with visible nostrils are not at all good with money. In these noses, the wings of the nose are not in line with the tip of the nose, and hence the nostrils look exposed. It is very difficult for these people to save money, because they have an extremely lax attitude when it comes to spending.

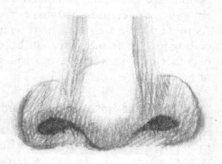

5. Wings of the Nose in line with the Tip

The wings of the nose are in line with the tip of the nose, i.e. they are in a straight line. In this case, the nostrils are fully covered and won't be visible at all. If the nostrils are not at all seen when looking at the nose from the side or front, it is considered extremely lucky in terms of wealth. These people are able to hold on to their finances and are very calculative when it comes to spending money. These people are also very detail-oriented and do not take things very lightly.

CATEGORISATION OF THE NOSE ACCORDING TO ITS ANGULAR POSITION

It is very important to look towards which side of the face the nose tip points while comparing the two sides. The nose can be either straight in the middle of the face, or slightly angled towards the left or right sides of the face. If it points towards one of the sides of the face, then that is where the inclination of the person lies. Now let us discuss all the three angular positions in detail:

1. Tip of the Nose exactly in the Middle of the Face

If the nose tip does not point noticeably towards the left or the right sides of the face, then this is a fairly balanced nose. This nose will always be straight down the middle of the face. These people are the most balanced among all, in their thoughts, emotions, preferences, actions, as well as other likes and dislikes. As these people are of an even temperament, they will treat each colleague as a friend, and will be equiposed towards everyone (whether men or women), and will not get involved in any group or sect.

2. Tip of the Nose Angled towards the Right

As has been mentioned before, the right side of the face is the male side, and the left side of the face is the female side. The nose is the major indicator of a person's personality as well as character, so people with their noses angled towards the right will have more male influences in their life, than female.

Women, whose noses angle towards the right, do not miss any opportunity of stimulating themselves sexually, whenever they encounter the male sex. Now, if the tip of the nose is angled to the right and if this person is a man, then this person is selfish.

3. Tip of the Nose Angled to the Left

If the tip of the nose is angled to the left, then this will represent a totally opposite case. These people will spend their finances more upon women. For example, men whose nose tip points towards the left are likely to spend more money upon females in their life, i.e. upon their wives, girlfriends, and other women for sexual purposes. Men whose nose points towards the left are desperate to have sexual encounters with women.

However, women in this category are more selfish and will be mostly concerned only about themselves. These women will also be biased against men.

CHAPTER 10

PHILTRUM

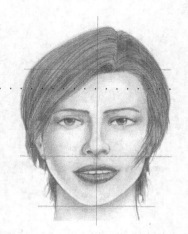

The philtrum is the vertical groove between the base of the nose and the middle part of the upper lip. Philtrum is a medical term given to this vertical groove and its etymological origins are traced to Greece — *philtron* or *philtre* are related to 'philanthropist' or 'philander', both of which relate 'to love' in one way or the other. The Greeks considered this part as erotic and a measure of sexual potency. In Vedic physiognomy, the philtrum indicates one's love life, sexual appetite, productivity, and physical constitution. The groove is like a bridge between the nose and the mouth, which are the sensory organs of smell, taste, and sex. The more noticeable the philtrum is, the more vitality a person has. The philtrum represents the middle part of a person's life, especially between the ages of 51-55 (most specifically 51).

While assessing this part of the face, it is very important to study five major aspects — length, breadth, depth, marks, and angular position. Now let us discuss all these aspects in detail.

CATEGORISATION OF THE PHILTRUM ACCORDING TO ITS LENGTH

1. Long Philtrum

A long philtrum is the ideal length or the moderate length of the philtrum, which is nearly two centimetres. People with a long

philtrum are well-endowed with life's forces. If the philtrum is long and deep, then these people are very romantic, sexual, lively and friendly. A long and deep philtrum is also an indicator of a good, long, fertile, fortunate, and healthy life. These people see consider-able advances in their fortune and personal status around the age of 50. However, it should be noted that this type of philtrum should not be unusually long because the person will be frustrated, will exhibit loss of reason, unusual behaviour, and a slothful nature. People with unusually long philtrums are governed by the mode of ignorance.

2. Short Philtrum

People with a short philtrum are generally inconsiderate. These people get easily captivated and carried away by attractive sexual partners, friends, or social groups. Every new idea which interests these people gives them a kind of thrill and excitement. Vedic

physiognomy is of the view that this type of philtrum is not conducive for a long life. These people sometimes do not even reach middle age. Also, if these people tend to live long, they might not have very good health through their life.

However, people with a short and deep philtrum are said to achieve remarkable success during their short lifespan. Even if these people do not become very famous and rich, they will very easily achieve the basic amenities of life at a very early age. Alexander the Great had such a philtrum, and conquered most of the known world at a very early age. Bruce Lee also had such a philtrum, he is famous worldwide as the greatest martial artist ever. Both Alexander and Bruce Lee died in their early thirties.

CATEGORISATION OF THE PHILTRUM ACCORDING TO ITS WIDTH

1. Wide Philtrum

People with a wide philtrum generally possess lots of sexual energy, especially if the philtrum is equally wide from top to bottom. These people become so sexual in their adult life that they shed all their inhibitions with the wish to enjoy their sex life to the fullest.

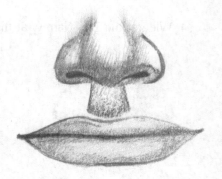

2. Deep and Wide Philtrum

People possessing a deep and wide philtrum will have the same sexual urge as people in the above category, however if the depth of the philtrum increases, the intensity and urge also increases.

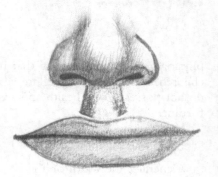

3. Narrow at the Top, Wide at the Bottom

This philtrum is shaped like a drop of water. Generally, philtrums are narrow at the top, and wide at the bottom. This indicates that the person will get involved in anything with his/her whole energy, including sexual activities, especially if this philtrum is very deep. The energy levels are very high in these people and they have lots of vitality and recuperative powers. They also utilise all their energy when working to give shape to their plans and are very strong-willed and positive-minded.

4. Wide at the Top, Narrow at the Bottom

If the philtrum is wide at the top and narrow at the bottom, it represents a lot of lust during childhood and younger days of life. This philtrum indicates that the person belongs to the category of people who prefer to experience sex at an early age. These people also suffer from low fertility so they will certainly have very few offsprings. Vedic physiognomy is of the view that these people do not have male children, and their offspring are certainly daughters. These people do not possess good health and are also deprived of wisdom and fortune.

5. Narrow Philtrum

Generally, the width of the philtrum should not be less than one centimetre. If the width of the philtrum is less than one centimetre then it is considered to be a narrow philtrum, and if the width is more than one centimetre then the philtrum should be considered to be a wide philtrum.

However, this width should be measured when the person is not smiling, because when the person smiles, the width of the philtrum increases by more than half an inch. A narrow philtrum indicates a very reserved nature. These people are not very open when it comes to discussing their issues with others. They will talk about their personal life only with those who are very close to them. These people also possess an orthodox view about sex. Even if some of them do not possess an orthodox view even then they will rarely be open to discussions about sex. They have a narrow view about dressing as well. Their health, vitality, and lifespan will also be major areas of concern.

6. Line Philtrum

If a person has such a narrow philtrum that the groove is represented by only a single line then these people will not have much when it comes to pleasure in their life. Their lives are very dry and they also lack resources for enjoyment. These people might also face some problems when they reach middle age. Health and finance will be their major areas of concern.

CATEGORISATION OF THE PHILTRUM ACCORDING TO ITS DEPTH

1. Deep Philtrum

People with a deep philtrum generally have abundant reserves of physical and sexual energy. These people generally perform well in sports and activities that require heavy physical work. They also need lots of sex to maintain their physical and

mental well-being. As these people are very hardworking and agile, their finances will be good. They possess good digestive systems as well as excellent appetites.

2. Flat Philtrum

A flat philtrum is an indication of one's weak constitution. These people are also very calculative and do not possess risk-seeking attitudes. Because of their weak life forces and drive, these people generally get nervous and disturbed very soon and also have a low sex drive. However, if this philtrum is broad then the person will not suffer from the ill-effects of a flat philtrum and will display all the features possessed by people with a wide philtrum.

3. Shallow Philtrum

Shallow philtrums are those that are not too deep, nor flat, nor too wide, but are moderately deep and wide, generally concave-shaped. People with shallow philtrums are good at saving money and creating future reserves. So, these people will have a stable future, in terms of finances. These people will have a refined sexual as well as professional life. They are also very balanced when it comes to enjoying different aspects of life, and also have good energy reserves.

4. Totally Smooth Upper Part/No Philtrum

In this case, the upper portion of the lip is totally smooth without any grooves; a philtrum won't be noticed on this face. These people generally possess fragile bodies. They will also undergo lots of health problems and might have to go through lots of emotional difficulties, especially because of constant conflicts in their love life. The sex drive of these people is also affected. According to Vedic physiognomy, this philtrum is not fortunate for the person as it indicates illness, loss of spouse, beloved and material assets, and in extreme cases, very early death.

5. Fading Philtrum

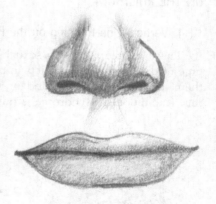

This type of philtrum is slightly different from the upper (no philtrum) category. This philtrum starts from the nose, but fades before reaching the mouth. Vedic physiognomy describes this type of philtrum as being extremely unfortunate. These people are sometimes said to be under a heavy influence of negative planets. They might become very successful, but unfortunate events will always affect them in some way. This philtrum also indicates loss of the spouse, or beloved. Illness as well as material losses are also indicated. These people might also have to live a solitary life during the later years of their life with deep turbulent feelings of isolation. They might also have trouble with their offspring.

6. Raised Philtrum

A raised philtrum has a raised middle part, i.e. the centre (which gives the philtrum a slightly convex look). Just look at the faces of monkeys, you will find this type of philtrum. People with such philtrums have abundant sexual energy and sex is a very vital part of their existence. If other features of their faces are auspicious then the abundant energy within them can make them able warriors, good sportsmen, good mechanics, and worthy in fields that require lots of physical effort, because these people are accustomed to heavy physical work.

CATEGORISATION OF THE PHILTRUM ACCORDING TO THE MARKS ON THE PHILTRUM

1. Vertical Line Running on the Philtrum

These people feel deep sexual lust. They also have an innate urge to display their sexual acts in public so that people can watch them, because they get abundant stimulation and satisfaction by this. Exhibitionism syndrome is quite common with these people.

It should be noted that this feature of public display of sexuality is also present in people with deep philtrums, as well as with people with wide and shallow philtrums, however that urge is not uncontrollable within them, but is uncontrollable within people with vertical lines upon their philtrums.

People with lines on their philtrum also have low

creativity levels as their minds are always engaged in gross sensuality and their minds are mostly dedicated towards sleaze. However, people with long, deep, and shallow philtrums are very creative. Most of the scientists, astronauts, and people in the creative field possess long, deep, and shallow philtrums.

2. Crooked Philtrum

If the philtrum is crooked, deformed, or if there are cut marks on the philtrum, then this is an indicator of a strong sexual appetite. These people are generally sexually frustrated and need lots of sex to satisfy their urges. If they are not able to quench their thirst for sex, then they might resort to unlawful ways to satisfy their lust, while others might end up living their lives in permanent frustration.

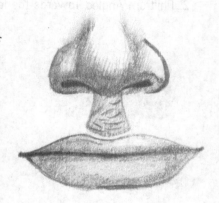

CATEGORISATION OF THE PHILTRUM ACCORDING TO ITS ANGULAR POSITION

1. Philtrum Angled Towards the right side of the Face

If the subject is female, this philtrum will cause deep frustration, as these women possess very strong desires to have male mates. These women might be sexually frustrated and so might adopt sex as their profession. Also this philtrum can lead to financial problems for these women, due to which they might become more desperate and frustrated.

These women will also use their sexual charisma very deliberately to impress people, especially for favours so that they can climb the ladder to success. In men, this kind of philtrum indicates some kind of conflict within their personal lives, most probably loss of direction, or very selfish behaviour.

2. Philtrum Angled Towards the left side of the Face

If the subject is female, a left angled philtrum represents selfishness, and an innate desire to get the most out of every situation. If the subject is male, then he might downplay sexuality in social situations. It should be noted that if the philtrum is angled towards the left, or the right sides of the face, it definitely affects the balance of the entire face, leading to an unbalanced personality. This might result in loss of direction, or depression due to failure, frustration, or financial problems. It also indicates that the person concerned might have to remain childless.

CHAPTER 11

. . . .

MOUTH

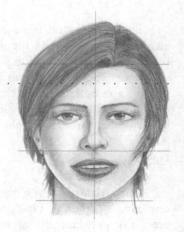

The mouth consists of the lips, teeth, tongue, as well as the whole of the mouth itself. So while assessing the mouth, it is very important to assess the lips, teeth, tongue, as well as the size and shape of the mouth as a whole. The mouth represents a person's mindset, personality, nature, and sensuality. You can judge whether a person is open-minded, or not, just by looking at their mouth. The mouth is also a major indicator of a person's mood and temperament. People who are warm and always in a good mood have a big mouth, because they always smile, which is the best indicator of a free-hearted person. On the contrary, people who are heavy hearted will always have a heavy and serious face and will most often possess small mouths. The mouth is also one of the major indicators of finance, so financial matters are also associated with the mouth, especially the lips.

Mercury rules the mouth, because this organ is related to speech and communication. The mouth is the basic indicator of how a person establishes the self with the public. Inauspicious mouths indicate that the planet Mercury is not placed in the right place in the natal chart. An auspicious mouth indicates the auspicious position of Mercury in the natal chart. People who have a good knowledge of face reading and who are generally very good at identifying people, generally avoid glancing at the mouth unless the person is smiling warmly.

Like the eyes and the eyebrows, the mouth can reveal several character traits such as the situation of a person in a particular mode, characteristic features like courage or cowardice, good, or evil nature etc. A mouth can indicate when someone tries to avoid you, or attempts to come close to you, or communicate verbally, or non-verbally. Now let's discuss all the features of the mouth one by one, starting with the lips.

LIPS

Apart from the eyes, the lips can help one determine how attractive a person is. Lips govern a person's sensual interests, and are major determinants of how giving, or selfish, a person is. As the eyes are the windows to the soul, likewise the lips are the windows to a person's personality, nature, and character. In behavioural science, one major feature that indicates one's good nature are the lips.

Lips determine our sexual appetites as well as our ability to nurture others in a loving relationship. In face reading, the lips and the mouth signifies how much luck the person will have at the age of 60. The lips are also one of the major indicators of finance. So, the lips should be clearly judged and seen.

Lips belong to different categories according to the size, thickness, colour, angular positions, lip proportions, as well as shapes. Let us discuss all these categories in detail.

LIP SIZE: CATEGORISATION OF THE LIPS ACCORDING TO THE SIZE OF THE LIPS

Lip size can determine one's personality, nature, character, and prosperity. Lips are divided into three basic categories, i.e. large lips, medium-length lips, and dainty lips.

1. Large Lips

Large lips indicate large personalities, as well as a voracious appetite for food, sex, and pleasure. These people are also very courageous, and possess a strong desire to live a luxurious life.

Most of the big lipped
people have a hedonistic
philosophy and approach
towards life. Some of them
might make friends very
easily because of their
generous nature. Big lipped
people are also very
outspoken and sometimes
might be very blunt as well.
If there are some other signs,
or marks on their face that
indicate a rebellious nature,
then these people will be very blunt.

Big lipped people do not have stage fright. These people are
very good at delivering public speeches. That's the reason most
entertainers and public personalities have large lips.

Also, big lipped people are very independent and daring, and
need lots of freedom, so very often they do not like to be held
back, or be confined to their homes. These people also like to be
in the limelight, so they always make an effort to get recognition.
They also like sex a lot, and sex is an important part of their life.
They generally possess voracious appetites when it comes to sex.

2. Medium Length

People whose lips are of
medium length are among
those who are strong willed,
humble, and polite. These
lips are neither as wide as
conventional mouths, nor are
they very small, but are
mediocre in length. These
people possess an even
temperament and are very
generous and expressive.
They are not hungry for
power, or the limelight, as

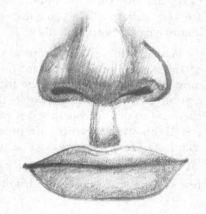

their large lipped counterparts. These people also possess a very rare quality of adjusting in any given situation and do not get easily worried. They never rush to conclusions, as most of them are well-balanced. People with medium length lips are flexible communicators when it comes to addressing a crowd, or dealing with one person.

3. Dainty Lips

People with small lips, probably less than an inch on both halves of the face i.e. the left and the right halves, are extremely self-centred. They do not have much tolerance when it comes to considering the other person's viewpoints. They are not very generous and are also inexpressive. They generally have lots of expectations from others and certainly want more from others materially, as well as emotionally. So, these people become easily annoyed, hypersensitive, if they do not get what they had in their mind, or what their perceptions were. So, you might see these people in a fit of anger or such emotions, every now and then. These people are very negative. They are not very trustworthy, because they themselves do not trust others.

People with very small lips also lack confidence and because of this, small lipped people are not good at public speeches, and most of them suffer from stage fright. Even if these people are in a group of three or more people, they cannot talk to others. They also tend to get nervous when speaking to people of the opposite sex. If no strong features are present upon their face, then they will live a life of poverty, and despondency.

Small lips very often suggest that the subjects will have only a few close acquaintances and will be lonely most of their life, especially after the age of 55. If other auspicious marks are not present on the face, then these people might live a miserable life.

CATEGORISATION OF THE LIPS ACCORDING TO THE THICKNESS OF THE LIPS

1. Thick Lips/Full Lips

People with thick lips are often very sensuous and dedicated to pleasure seeking. These people love food and are voracious eaters. They also possess a lusty nature, because of their love for sex. Thick lips are also indicators of a warm personality. If the other marks on the face are good then they will be very generous and will treat others with warmth.

Lip fullness is related to how frank or revealing a person is. It's about self disclosure. You will find many thick lipped people sharing themselves (their ideas, personalities, characteristics, emotions) with the world. If the subject is a female and she is in good shape, just give her any costume or garment and she will wear it graciously, even if the garments are very revealing. You will find that most of the women who strip for fashion magazines or do the job of strippers are full lipped (and full figured).

Vedic physiognomy is of the opinion that women with fuller lips have high oestrogen levels, which makes them highly-sexed individuals. Oestrogen also helps in breast formation and in development and maintenance of female characteristics of the body, so you will find that most women with fuller lips have full round breasts and a nice curvaceous body. A high level of oestrogen in females is also related to health and fertility, so women with full lips are also very healthy, fertile, sensual, and sexy and hence are most often sought by the male sex.

So full lips indicate that a person is comfortable with one's own identity, however if the lips are very exaggeratedly thick, it indicates an exaggeration in the person's attitude, lifestyle, and expression. People with very thick lips are so comfortable with themselves that they don't mind embarrassing others and embarrassing themselves as well, in certain situations. Their character and behaviour will most often be unpredictable.

2. Pouting Lips

Pouting lips are bow-shaped thick lips, with the ends pointing upwards. The upper as well as lower lips are thick and the upper lips are shaped like a bow, giving a very sensuous look to the lips. The sexual appetite of these people is very strong. These people are prone to indulging excessively in sex. They also demand love and affection and need constant nourishment during their childhood as well. Apart from sex, these people also tend to indulge in food and wine, as people with thick lips enjoy delicious food. These lips are also indicators of good health, finance, intelligence, and lasting friendships.

Pouting lips also indicate an immature emotional streak in the character. These people, especially young women, are most often prone to sulking and throwing tantrums. These women are also fickle-minded, which results in a constant change in their moods.

In women, these lips are indicators of high oestrogen levels, hence you will find the most sexy and sensual women in this category, especially in the glamour industry. If other features of their faces are good then these people will have excellent financial reserves.

3. Thin Lips

Thin lipped people are very cautious. Thin lips also indicate a very dominating and controlling nature. These people like to have full control over everything. If the lips are thin and wide, then these people like to take command of everything around them and are extremely bossy. Because of their

dominating, controlling and cautious nature, these people will definitely not like someone talking about their personal life, or teasing them about something. These people are not generous, are very calculative and most often possess a selfish temperament.

4. Pursed Lips

People whose lips seem to be clenched inside their mouth possess very mean, wicked, and vile natures. These people are extremely selfish, and self-centred. They are only concerned about themselves and their own needs and wants. They will try to fulfil their own desires, with complete disregard to others. These people also possess revengeful and harmful natures and might harm others even at the slightest pretext. People with such lips are also very stubborn.

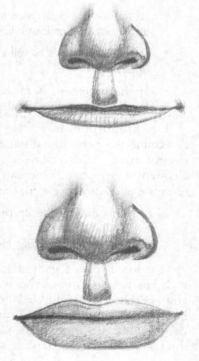

5. Moderate Thickness

According to Vedic physiognomy, the lips that are of moderate thickness, i.e. neither too thick, nor too thin, are considered to be the best among all. People with lips of moderate thickness possess even temperaments, fine, and adjustable natures. Also, they do not speak too much, or uselessly, and are not accustomed to concealing anything. These people are also very family-oriented and love and support their families. They will never display excessiveness in eating, sleeping, or mating, and are very balanced.

LIP PROPORTIONS

This categorisation of the lips is done according to the proportion of the upper to the lower lip. To read lip proportions, the comparison between the fullness of the upper and the lower lip needs to be done.

- Very commonly it is observed that the lower lip is somewhat fuller than the upper lip. This lip type is called moderately fuller lower lip.

- If the lower lip is twice as full as the upper one, then the lip is extra-fuller lower lip.

- If the upper lip is as full as the lower lip, this is called fuller upper lip.

- If the upper lip is more full and pronounced than the lower lip, then this is called the extra-fuller upper lip.

Lip proportion is a very important subject that helps determine the behavioural pattern of human beings in a social environment. It also plays a major role in ascertaining how eloquent a person is. One can also determine how important objective and subjective things are to a person.

Now let us discuss the lip proportions in detail.

1. Moderately Fuller Lower Lip

The lower lip is slightly fuller than the upper lip. People with such lips belong to the balanced category. The person's thoughts and speeches are highly balanced. This person tends to think before he/she speaks and does not like to be rushed to conclusions. People with a slightly fuller lower lip are also interested in learning about anything that seems to be very interesting. These people like to discuss a lot about different things, such as the different aspects of life, like religion, science, beliefs etc. Such people are very enthusiastic, since they are simply interested in every aspect of life.

2. Extra-Fuller Lower Lip

The lower lip is twice as full as the upper lip. The Vedic texts say that these lips possess the quality to arouse extreme emotions. These lips are known for the gift of gab. These people do not need to force you to do something, but you will be compelled to agree with whatever they say. This vibration increases more if these people have lotus eyes, or trance eyes, with an auspicious central axis and third eye region. Believe it or not, most of the influential speakers throughout the world have such lips. If you try to notice people very closely, you will be amazed to see that most influential news readers, journalists, as well as writers have such lips.

However, it should be noted that if the person possesses these lips and does not have other auspicious features on his/her face, then this characteristic can also become detrimental to one's personality, character, and destiny. These people will be grossly sensual, unlucky in love, unreliable, and very egoistic. They have very high opinions about themselves. Some lower lips are so thick that they seem to be bulging out. These lips are most probably three or four times thicker than the upper lips. These lips destroy the beauty of the lips and make the face look very awkward. These lips take away all the auspicious qualities of the person and people with such lips are grossly foolish, crude sensualists, brash in their behaviour, and useless.

3. Full Upper Lip

If the upper lip of a person is fuller in the way that the upper and the lower lip are equal in breadth and size, then it should be considered that the upper lip is fuller than normal. These people will possess the same sensuality and romanticism as possessed by people with thick lips. However, it should be noted that in Vedic face reading, the significance of the upper lip is that the upper lip provides control and the significance of the lower lip is that it provides farsightedness, visualisation, or intuition powers. So the Vedic scholars are of the opinion that the upper lip should always be thinner than the lower lip so that the person should have proper control over his body, mind, senses, and action. So, the fuller the upper lip becomes, the looser the gravity, control or hold becomes. People, whose upper lips are thicker, are sometimes said to lose control over their minds and emotions and tend to flow with their desires.

4. Extra-Full Upper Lip

If the upper lips are thicker than the lower ones, then these lips are in the category of extra-full upper lips. People in this category tend to be very shrewd and very selfish. These people pretend to be great lovers, but do not really love the person. They pretend to be in love, to fulfil their own needs and wants. These people are certainly not the way they project themselves. Their real nature comes out as soon as they feel that they have nothing to take from you. An extra fuller upper lip is also an indicator of a difficult childhood.

DIFFERENT TYPES OF LIPS

This section will explain the different types of lips and how to interpret the inner natures, personality, and destiny of a person by studying the lips.

1. Lined Lips

Some people have lots of lines on their lips. If there are not many lines then they will at least have some lines on their lips, especially one line on the middle part of their upper or lower lip. These people are very careful with money and are among those who tread very softly. They will properly consider the pros and cons of everything before they strike the final

deal. While speaking with someone, they speak the right things at the right time. Please don't confuse the lined lip people with the dry lip people. Lined lip people have permanent lines upon their lips, the dry lip people will have lines upon their lips because of dryness. However, if the lips are dry and lined, then these people will become very selfish and mean, and will be concerned only about themselves. They believe in taking advantage of each and every person and situation. Most of the lined lip people are also very greedy, covert, and selfish.

2. Oval Lips

These lips have rounded corners which gives a horizontal oval shape to the lips. These people are slightly slow in decision making, but once they have made a decision, they become

thoughtless and abruptly execute their decisions. They are also very sensual, as their lips always tend to be full and round. These people also tend to be very cynical, and confused. The indications of wealth for these people are very good, however they should take care of their money.They also try to achieve success through shortcuts, as they do not possess too much patience and are cynical about going about it the long way, or working hard. Full round lips also mean an extrovert personality, so these people also possess the nature of self-disclosure. These lips are not possessed by so-called shy people as these people reveal themselves.

3. Hexagonal Lips

These lips are shaped like a hexagon. You can easily count all the six sides because these lips generally have pointed ends. Their mouths never make an upward or downward curve. These people are very orderly, logical, and balanced thinkers. They also possess an unconventional outlook towards sex, romanticism, and life. These lips are very auspicious for money and financial matters. However, people whose mouths are squarish, are wicked and deceptive.

4. Chipped Lips

Sometimes, the mouth remains half-open, or slightly open and

you can see the teeth even
when the mouth is closed. It
seems as if small sections of
both the upper and lower lips
are missing, which does not
allow the mouth to close
properly. This indicates some
kind of negative disturbances
in these people's life during
their childhood, or in their
early teens. Also, there could
be some kind of negative

disturbances in their life after the age of fifty. These people are
also sometimes very sarcastic and enjoy mockery, sarcasm and the
denigration of others.

5. Distorted or Crooked Lips

These people are not fair,
or genuinely honest. Their
character has a few grey
shades. Vedic physiognomy
explains that people with
crooked mouths have crooked
thoughts and a weak character.

6. Downward Curved Lips/Hanging Lips

There are some people who
possess downward curved lips, in
which one or both the lips hang
downwards, and the mouth
resembles that of the monkey. As
these lips resemble those of the
monkey, so is their behaviour and
character. These people are
extremely untrustworthy, as they

utter trivial lies about every small issue. The habit of fibbing is so prominent that even while having a normal conversation, they cannot live without boasting about themselves. They always pretend to be greater than they usually are.

People with lips that turn down, might also have had an unhappy and rocky childhood. However people whose mouth resembles that of a monkey, or goat, will be financially stable during the later years of life. Some of them might also be rich and affluent (if other features are auspicious). Most of these people are pleasure seekers. Curved lips also indicate that the subject is very self-centred and cares very little about what others think. Women with such lips possess questionable characters.

7. Dimpled Lips/Pointed Corners

These people generally have dimples at the edges of their mouths. These dimples are in the form of little indents at the outer edges of the mouth. People with dimples or pointed outer lip corners have a fierce desire for a lovable partner. These people are fiercely attracted towards the opposite sex and are always looking for a lovable partner. They are also very sexual. These people are also very delicate and sensitive. Their bodies and emotions are so sensitive to outside stimuli that they, especially women get immediately aroused by any kind of external stimulation like a soft touch, embrace, whisper in their ears, or any kind of erotic conversation.

8. Asymmetrical Lips

As the name itself suggests, the person's lips and personality will have some kind of asymmetry.

Both sides of the lips, i.e. the left and the right sides, are not symmetrical. One side of the lip might be slightly shorter than the other side. One side of the lip might be crooked, slightly thicker, thinner, etc. People with such lips have a mixed personality. This person will also experience some kind of major illness between 53-60 years of age, due to which he/she might become very weak. The characters and traits of both men and women possessing such asymmetrical lips should be determined as per the symptoms of the lip asymmetry like the length, thickness, angular positions of both sides of lips etc.

9. Bow-Shaped Lips

Generally the lips should be shaped like a bow, as bow-shaped lips are very auspicious for the person who possesses them. Bow-shaped lips are created by a low dipping point in the middle of the upper lip, while the ends point upwards. The low dipping point in the middle of the upper lip is also called the point of refinement. People with such lips have a refined taste. They are also lovers of beauty and art. These people have a sharp intellect and will use refined words with elegance and style, which penetrates deep inside one's minds, hearts, and souls, just like the bow shoots an arrow and penetrates its target.

These people possess a unique gift of gab. They are very influential and possess a unique grace and style. These lips are auspicious for each and every profession, especially for politics, administration, creativity, and arts. Also, if the middle of the upper lip is shaped like a rosebud, then that will enhance the person's power, ability, artistic, and romantic nature.

SOME OTHER SPECIAL CHARACTERISTICS OF THE LIPS AND THEIR SIGNIFICANCE

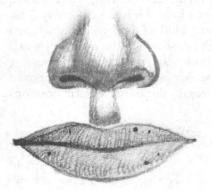

1. Pimples on the Lips

There are many people who have pimples or boils on their upper or lower lip. These pimples come on the lips because of lots of heat in the stomach. This happens mostly due to indigestion and daily constipation.

2. Dry Lips

As told earlier, dry lips should not be compared with lined lips as dry lips are indicators of completely different personality traits. Dry lips are permanently coarse and rough due to dryness. Permanent dry lips are indicators of a vile, mean, and degraded person. These people are also lifeless, and are least interested in any endeavour. They also possess the 'passing the buck' attitude and hence waste their lives on futile and useless things that bring no good results.

Dry lips are also indicators of a bad stomach. These people do not have a proper digestive system and hence most of the food remains undigested which in turn produces lots of toxins. These people have lots of unutilised fire in their stomach, which often causes the dryness of their lips. Most people who are heavy smokers and drinkers also have dry lips because of the excessive presence of the fire element in their body.

CATEGORISATION OF LIPS ACCORDING TO THEIR ANGULAR POSITION

1. Angled Upwards/Crescent Lips

Crescent lips have the shape of a waning, or half moon, in which the lips are generally curved upwards in the form of a semi-circle. These people possess good humour and are fun-loving. They are also lovers of beauty and art and generally tend

to work well in creative fields.
They are also likable and
generous individuals and tend
to cope with difficult
situations in a spirited way.
They laugh and smile a lot
and cope with problems by
smiling and not getting too
bothered about problems.
These people are certainly
very optimistic and have a lot
of positive energy within

them. However these people are also very demanding and
exacting and have a very clever personality. They are also good at
faking their emotions so they might not always represent their
true selves and thoughts in front of people.

2. Angled Downwards/Drooping Lips

People whose lips curve
downwards think they are
great perfectionists and it
becomes very difficult for
these people to admit their
own shortcomings. They
also like gossiping about
others, so you will see
them gossiping about others,
rather than talking about
themselves. Once these
people have got what they

want from someone, they don't even bother to talk to that person
properly.

Some of these people will also spend a lot of time on higher
education and will have a very unconventional lifestyle. They
might rely on others for financial support.

People with downward angled lips also tend to be negative
thinkers. So, whenever these people start a new project, or are
negotiating a deal with someone, they always keep the negative
aspects (of that project or deal) in their mind, and do not get

disappointed very much, when things turn out to be negative.

3. Straight Lips

Straight lips are those that are in a straight horizontal line and are neither angled upward, nor downwards. Straight-lipped people are very practical and methodical. These people have a lot of self-control and possess the stamina to undergo severe penances for higher causes. They are also very straightforward and deliberate.

As these people are very practical, they will never over-judge or undermine a particular situation under any circumstances. This means that these people will properly chalk out the negative and the positive sides of a plan before working on it, and will neither be over optimistic, or very pessimistic about the results of that plan.

4. Unevenly Angled Lips

Unevenly angled lips are those in which one side of the lip is angled upwards and the other side of the lip is angled downwards or straight. However, to correctly see which side of the lip is angled in which direction, a person should always judge a person's face when the person is not smiling because it is generally seen that the left lip (or in some cases right) is always angled upwards slightly when a person smiles. On the other hand, if the left lip of a man is permanently angled upwards, or when he is talking then this should be seen as a sign of his lust for women.

In cases where the man's right side of the lip is angled upwards (while speaking or otherwise), it indicates some kind of constant internal conflict. Their heads tell them something while their hearts tell them something different. Again, these men might also tend to be homosexuals.

This case will be totally opposite if the subject is a woman. In women, if the left lip is angled upwards and the right lip is angled downwards then the concerned woman is a pretender and is also a hardcore materialist. These women tend to be hypocrites so they generally speak and project something else to the outer world. These women also tend to be very selfish, shrewd, and cunning and are great manipulators of words.

In cases where a woman's right lip is angled upwards and the left lip is angled downwards, she does not tend to be happy from within and might sometimes be depressed.

LIP LINES

Lip lines are formed between both the lips when the lips are closed and are touching each other. These lines might have straight ends, ends pointing downwards, or pointing upwards. All of these three conditions have a specific meaning and significance. Let's discuss these three conditions in detail.

1. Ends turned Downwards

These people are sarcastic and always try to find out faults in each and everything. These people rarely see the positive side of the story, as they are very pessimistic. So, if you are starting a new project or an enterprise and you wish to know all the  possible dangers regarding that project, consult these people because no one is better than them in explaining the negative side of the story. These people are also not good at keeping promises. They will experience turbulent times, usually after the age of 40.

2. Ends Turned Upwards

These people are optimists. They can see the best even in the worst conditions. However, the drawback to this is that they tend to ignore the negative aspects of a plan. So they might have to face losses in the long run if they do not learn to acknowledge the negative facets as well.

While consulting or negotiating a business deal with them, it should always be kept in mind that they always try to present a rosy picture, even about the worst things in life. Hence, most people who cheat others with false promises have lip lines turned upwards, as they can easily present a wonderful picture of even the worst things. A positive feature of these people is that they are positive all the time, and do not break down easily.

3. Straight Ends

People with straight lip lines, i.e. with ends neither turned upwards nor down-wards, have poise, and dignity. They do not believe in highlighting anything too much, irrespective of whether the thing is positive or negative and will always work towards their goals without uselessly getting involved in too much gossip.

They also possess balanced personalities and have a balanced outlook. They do not draw a very positive or negative picture for the future, and see things as they are.

COLOUR OF THE LIPS

The colour of the lips plays a vital role in determining the health and personality of a person. Let us discuss what the colour of the lips signifies.

Red or Pink Lips

Red or pink lips have a very interesting history in the Vedic context, and most people are unaware of this. It is a scientific fact that whenever the blood rushes into the lips, the lips immediately become red. It can also be noted that when people are sexually aroused, or just after a sexual activity, the lips tend to become red. In ancient India, young women used to redden their lips whenever they were about to meet their beloved, just to indicate that they were sexually aroused. It used to be a signal that they have intense feelings for their beloved. However, nowadays, you will see that almost every woman reddens her lips, without knowing the exact meaning, or the philosophy behind it.

These people possess very good health, vitality, and potency. People with red lips are full of life, very adventurous, excited, and hardworking. They also possess a deep love for their friends, spouses, and family. People with red lips live life like kings.

Colourless Lips

Generally lips tend to be either red or pink. People who have a darker complexion will have lips that are dark too. But, if the lips are neither red, nor pink, nor of the colour and texture of the skin and are colourless, then these lips have a different meaning altogether. People with colourless lips very often lack emotional stability, and physical vitality. These people also do not have a lot of interest for new endeavours and possess a weak mental and emotional constitution. Most of these people do not possess very sharp minds and are very reluctant to study, or work in any field.

These people also lack sexual potency and might have to undergo a lot of difficulty to produce a male child (if they wish to have one), as most of them are infertile. People with colourless, or rough lips, find pleasure and enjoyment in bad company.

SIZE OF MOUTHS

The size of the mouth has a very important role in face reading as it helps determine the type of personality, temperament, and wealth of a person.

1. Big Mouths/Lion Mouth

The sizes of these mouths are very large. That's the reason these mouths are compared with the mouth of the lion. Just like a lion can hold its prey in its mouth, irrespective of the size of the prey, likewise big mouthed people can keep big objects inside their mouths easily.

These mouths are also very good indicators of good health and vitality. People with such mouths rarely fall sick as they have a highly developed immune system and are tough. They also possess voracious appetites, when it comes to food and sex. One way to identify these people is to see the way they eat their food. They will generally take large bites, eat quickly, and finish their meals very quickly. These people are definitely not shy, and are very outgoing and outspoken in their nature and behaviour.

Some of the Vedic face readers are of the opinion that these people might be struck by ill-fortune. However, if other features on their face are auspicious then these people might hold wealth, power, and influence in their lives.

2. Small Mouths

Generally small mouthed people lack guts and enthusiasm and are filled with fear and negative emotions from inside, hence they generally live an average life, or below average life, some of them might not even possess the basic amenities.

These people are generally not able to work for longer periods, and do not have the patience and stamina to work for long hours, and hence they do not get very good results in their endeavours. They are also not competitive and generally hold others responsible for their own pathetic condition. Small mouths generally indicate a greedy, quarrelsome, and wicked nature. These people are not very giving, so in personal relationships they generally cause unnecessary chaos. Most of these women are not able to produce sons.

3. Average Size Mouths

Average size mouths are always lucky. People with average mouths are neither as voracious as the bigger mouth ones, nor as greedy and thrifty as their smaller mouthed counterparts. These people possess even mindsets. They are also gentle and precise. People with average size mouths won't be spendthrifts and as outspoken, wild, impetuous, as the bigger mouthed ones, nor will they be very cunning, quarrelsome, bereaving, and as destitute as the smaller mouthed counterparts.

These mouths are very good indicators of fortune and destiny. These people usually live a luxurious life and money comes to them quite naturally, if other signs of their faces are also auspicious. They will also hold powerful positions in their area of business, if other features of their faces are good. Most of the people with average mouths are very rich and influential.

TEETH

Teeth have a very important role in face reading. The setting of the teeth is a very important factor in determining and judging the temperament, nature, and character of a person. Beautiful white teeth that are evenly placed inside the mouth are considered to be auspicious in Vedic physiognomy. People with shining, white, pearl-like teeth that are evenly placed inside the mouth are lucky, wealthy, and powerful. Crooked teeth that are yellow or black, which have gaps between them are considered to be inauspicious. It should be noted that Saturn rules the teeth, so faulty teeth indicate an inauspicious placement of Saturn in the natal chart. Now let's discuss the outcomes of the different types of teeth upon the personality, nature, and character of the individual.

1. Even Teeth with no Gaps between Them

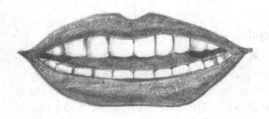

If the teeth of a person are even in shape and size and there are no gaps between any two teeth, and the teeth are closely placed touching each other on the sides, then this is the perfect place-ment of the teeth. These people are even minded and possess even temperaments. They are also benevolent and generally care about the other person's needs and wants as well. These people do not rush into decisions quickly and are very practical, methodical, and deliberate in their actions.

2. Uneven Teeth

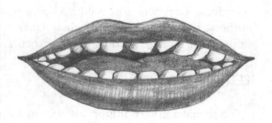

Uneven teeth are generally possessed by those who do not have even temperaments and are very fickle minded. These people also possess base, mean, and faulty natures. They usually possess wicked dispositions if there are gaps between their teeth. These teeth indicate the presence of animalistic dispositions. Just observe the teeth of any animal and you will be amazed to see that all of them have uneven teeth. These teeth also indicate uneven lives and heavy bumps ahead in life.

3. Spaced Teeth

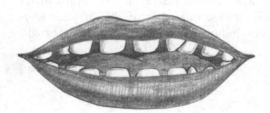

Spaced teeth have gaps between them. People with such teeth possess a n i m a l i s t i c dispositions. They possess base natures and are extremely selfish, wicked, mean, harmful, and vile. They are among those who live only for themselves and who do not give importance to moral considerations.

Vedic physiognomy considers that people who possess gaps between their teeth or people with uneven teeth are among those who have the characteristics of demons. If you look at the ancient sculptures or paintings in India, you will be amazed to see that in all the ancient sculptures and paintings, the demons are shown as having uneven teeth with lots of gaps between their teeth.

4. Spaced Front Teeth

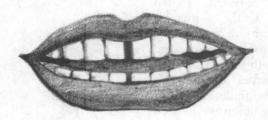

If there are gaps between the front two teeth, especially between the upper front two teeth, then this indicates an extremely cheap and foolish nature, irrespective of whether the other teeth (in the mouth) are also spaced apart from each other or not. Space between the front two teeth indicates a daredevil who likes taking risks and is outrageous and outspoken.

5. Big Front Teeth

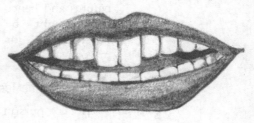

If the upper front two teeth (or sometimes lower) are much bigger in size than the rest then this indicates that the person is impatient and extremely stubborn.

6. Inward Bending Teeth

Inward bending teeth indicates a poor life. These people are constantly in strife with the world. Their minds are greatly disturbed by the thoughts as to who is good, who is bad, what

should be done, what's not to be done etc. These people do not possess peace of mind and their heads and hearts are also in constant strife. They also possess sarcastic dispositions, are extremely sexual and might also possess a sadistic or a masochistic disposition. These people are also hostile. Women in this category will possess questionable characters.

7. Outward Angled Teeth

People with outward angled teeth possess more or less the same nature and character like those with inward bending teeth. These people possess questionable characters and also like finding faults in others. They are very defensive as well and because of this attitude, they might be struggling against the world and within themselves.

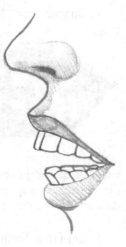

These people also possess hostile natures and hence they might be sadistic, or masochistic.

8. Sharp Canine Teeth/Lion Teeth

If a person has sharp canine teeth resembling a lion, then this is representative of a determined person. These people are very courageous and strong willed. Once these people decide something and have undertaken a particular project, they generally do not back down unless and until they completely finish the job. So there are good indications of success for them. These people might become successful at an early age and might reach prominence in their careers immediately after marriage.

9. Cavities in the Teeth

Generally people think that cavities in the teeth are because of the result of not taking proper care of the teeth and because of eating lots of sweets. However, people do not know that it has a lot to do with face reading as well. In face reading, healthy teeth are generally considered to be auspicious and cavities in the teeth indicate certain traits.

Firstly, people with teeth cavities are extremely pleasure seeking. They possess intense sexual and sensual natures so whatever they do, they do it for pleasure. Secondly, as these people are pleasure loving they generally do not eat to live; they live to eat, as pleasure loving people are far away from a disciplined life. Thirdly, most of the people with cavities are also affected by sloth. Most of these people are also addicted to pornography. Almost all women in the porn industry will have cavities in their teeth.

NUMBER OF TEETH

The way the teeth are placed in the mouth, as well as the number of teeth a person possesses has a direct relationship to the quality of life a person will generally live. So if possible, the number of teeth possessed by an individual should be clearly determined to conclude about the subject's life and destiny.

1. Thirty-two Teeth

People with thirty-two teeth generally have sixteen in each line, i.e. sixteen on the upper part, and sixteen on the lower. This even calculation means that the person is generally fortunate. These people are generally balanced, and do not work in haste, or under pressure. They are generally very calculative, methodical, and deliberate and will not like to rush themselves. This even number of teeth is also considered good for business and entrepreneurship because these people have a sound temperament for handling the various facets of business. Most people in this category who possess other auspicious features as well, will be wealthy.

2. Thirty-three or Thirty-one Teeth

If the subject possesses thirty-one or thirty-three teeth then due to the odd number of teeth, the subject will generally have an uneven temperament. These people are hardcore materialists, and most of them might also possess a hedonistic approach towards life.

It should also be kept in mind that if the number of teeth is less than thirty-one then this is the sure sign of cruelty, and bad luck.

3. More Teeth in the Lower Jaw than the Upper

If the individual's lower jaw has more teeth than the upper one then this is the sign of bad luck. These people undergo severe sufferings in life and as already stated, an odd number of teeth are never auspicious.

TONGUE

The tongue is a very important part of our mouth and is an amazing muscle. The tongue allows a person to taste, to enjoy kissing, and sex and to move the food in the mouth. It also helps lubricate the food so that it can be easily chewed and swallowed. The tongue also plays an important role in our accent and speech. Without the tongue, it would be very difficult to speak.

Let's discuss the significance of the different types of tongues in face reading.

CATEGORISATION OF THE TONGUE ACCORDING TO ITS LENGTH

The length of the tongue determines and judges the physical prowess, vitality, and energy of a person. It also helps us get an overview of the financial status of a person. The length of the tongue is very important and determines how spiritual and metaphysical a person is, or how attached the person is to this material world.

1. Long Tongue

A long tongue is considered to be very auspicious in Vedic physiognomy. A long tongue is the basic indicator of a person's physical vitality and spiritual soundness. It is generally

considered that if a person's tongue reaches till his chin when that person elongates his/her tongue, then it should be considered that this person has the ideal tongue length. Just see the statue of Goddess Kali, her tongue extends below her chin. Men with a longer tongue are considered to have fertile sperm and are said to produce children with great talents. People with longer tongues also possess excellent health. These tongues also indicate that there will be no dearth of finances for such a person.

2. Short Tongue

A short tongue belongs to the hardcore earthly materialists. People with short tongues are never able to stretch or elongate their tongue too far out. Their tongue will never reach the chin and will only reach half the way. However as it is said, practice makes man perfect, so keep trying, you might be able to make it.

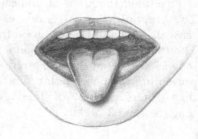

CATEGORISATION OF THE TONGUE ACCORDING TO ITS WIDTH

1. Narrow Tongue

A narrow tongue is the indicator of cruelty and the presence of negative character traits.

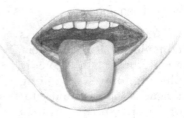

Narrow Tongue   Wide Tongue

2. Wide Tongue

A wide and tender tongue indicates benevolent and sympathetic natures. These people are generally good-hearted and possess a deep love for mankind. Most of them will involve themselves in charity, trusts etc, and will be keen to help others in every possible way, as per their capacity.

CATEGORISATION OF THE TONGUE ACCORDING TO ITS COLOUR

1. Pink Tongue

The pink tongue is an indicator of good health and vitality. These people possess good sexual powers and are definitely sensual. They also possess good mannerisms and speak graciously. The tongue determines the kind of speech, so people with pink tongues will definitely have a refined and regal way of talking and presenting their viewpoint. These people definitely live longer than others because of their good health. People with pink tongues are full of life.

2. Black Tongue

A black tongue, or a black spot on the tongue is inauspicious. These people possess extremely fragile bodies, and bad health. They might need to be hospitalised frequently, for some issues, because of their health. They are also prone to infections and diseases. Most of the people with a black tongue will also have a very thin and bony body, with hollowed or sunken cheeks and lots of lines upon their face, which often seems to show that these people are lifeless and do not have a great enthusiasm about life. These people might live desolate and enslaved lives.

Black tongues are also indicators of extra-sensory perceptions of the wrong kind. This means that these people use their sixth sense to predict wrong outcomes for others. Many people possessing black tongues might also become involved in black magic and other wicked things because they get pleasure by exploiting and harming others.

It should also be noted that the tongue is ruled by Mercury in the natal chart, so a faulty tongue indicates the inauspicious position of Mercury in the natal chart.

3. White Tongue

A white tongue indicates that a person is dehydrated. These people might not be accustomed to drinking a lot of water and might also have stomach disorders as well. Such people also suffer from bad breath. This also happens because of lack of water and because of undigested and rotten food in the stomach. Women who stay at home and are not physically very active often suffer from this problem. People who are accustomed to smoking, or drinking a lot, are also prone to these problems.

4. Rough and Abrasive Tongue

If the upper layer of the tongue is rough and abrasive then it is generally not considered good for the person who possesses it. Such a tongue is generally possessed by lions, tigers, and other carnivore animals whose upper layer of the tongue are like rough thorns which helps them lick and devour the flesh of their prey. People with rough and abrasive tongues possess a quarrelsome and wicked temperament. These people are very hostile and selfish. They will generally create big problems for others, even at the slightest offence. These people also possess voracious appetites, so no matter how much others do for them, they won't get easily satisfied and will always hanker for more.

PALATE

Generally the palate of a person should be pink, soft, and smooth to indicate good fortune. A rough, coarse, and dry palate indicates bad-fortune and health. People with a rough, coarse, and dry palate do not succeed in life, no matter how hard they try. They will always lack good luck and fortune, and will have to struggle a lot in their lives. If the palate is black then also the person will live a miserable life. These people also destroy their race and family. Women with black coloured palates are affected with ill-fortune and do not portray wisdom, fine speech, virtue, chastity, and fortune. These women generally enjoy the company of ill-mannered and unchaste people, who are quarrelsome. If the palate is fleshy, black, coarse, and dry then these people's wealth is wasted and they generally choose the wrong path and lead miserable lives.

CHAPTER 12

. . . .

CHEEKS AND CHEEKBONES

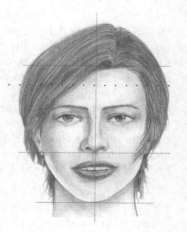

The cheeks determine how authoritative, dominant, or easygoing a person is. Cheeks also suggest how bold, adventurous, and sensual a person is. So, it is very important to know what kind of cheeks and cheekbones a person has. Cheeks are formed on the face where the cheekbones lie. So, if the cheekbones are very high, then the cheeks will also be high, if the cheekbones are close to the nose, the cheeks will also be formed close to the nose while smiling or laughing. Now it should be noted that if the person has a very sculpted face, the cheeks and cheekbones can be very clearly determined, but, if there is a lot of fat in the body and the face, and if the skin sags, then the cheeks might hang down, even if the person has high and prominent cheekbones. In these cases, one should determine the exact position of the cheeks when the person is laughing, because at that moment the flesh or the fat of the cheek is formed at the correct place. One can even touch the face of the person to determine the exact position of the cheekbones.

Cheeks help determine the quality of life during the age groups 46-47. Apart from these age groups, the type and placement of cheeks and cheekbones are major factors in determining the nature and character of a person, so the quality of a person's life throughout his/her life will be affected by the type of cheeks and cheekbones a person has. The quality of life at 46 is determined by the left cheek, and at 47 is determined by the right cheek.

An important fact about cheeks is that it is believed that a fleshy face means that the person is obese. This is absolutely incorrect. A full face does not always mean obesity. It should be noted that this has more to do with the padding of the cheeks. If you observe different faces, you will very easily conclude that there are many people who are very skinny but still have full faces, and there are those who are very obese, but still have meagre padding on their cheeks. It should also be noted that fuller cheeks are considered to be more auspicious in Vedic face reading than hollowed, skinny, or bony cheeks.

Cheek padding also indicates the way a person handles position and power. Vedic physiognomy mentions that those with bigger cheek padding are softer, more benevolent, and more democratic in power games. However, people with small cheeks show a completely different style of handling position and power. They are more autocratic. Once they have made a decision, they are least interested in the other person's opinions and viewpoints. People feel more threatened with the way these people handle power, as they thrive on doing things alone, and delegating everything as per their wishes. Small cheeks also indicate vanity, false pride, jealousy, and a tendency to dominate others.

This doesn't mean that people should start eating a lot, or use artificial means to increase one's cheeks, because if a person with small cheeks padding starts eating a lot and becomes fat, the facial muscles are also bound to increase and become fat. That won't mean that the person has become very democratic, or benevolent in his/her outlook. Vedic physiognomy stresses more upon the overall construction of the face (and the body). This will become clearer, as we proceed further with detailed descriptions of different types of cheeks and cheekbones.

DIFFERENT TYPES OF CHEEKS AND CHEEKBONES

1. High and Prominent

Cheeks that are high and prominent suggest that the person is commanding in nature. The prominence of the cheek indicates leadership styles, so these people are very aggressive, authoritative, and sometimes very domineering, especially if other marks on their face also indicate an authoritative nature. These people always love to be in the limelight, that's the reason you will find many stars and performers have such cheeks. Like their cheeks, these people's personalities also stick out in the crowd. In face reading, prominent cheeks or cheekbones are not at all considered good for women, especially with regard to family issues. These women will not have good personal relationships and their private lives will be in turmoil. The

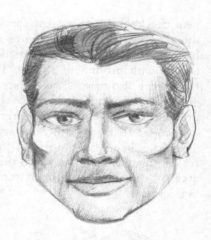

chances of negative disturbances increase if these women have high foreheads as well. That's because high cheekbones indicate aggression and competitiveness, and a very high forehead indicates power. So, these women do not make desirable mates.

However, in today's world, if you turn the pages of any fashion magazine, you will be amazed to find that 90% of female models have high cheekbones and high foreheads, and maybe clefts on the tip of their nose. It will be a very big challenge for these women to balance their personal and professional lives.

Prominent cheeks are good for models because they need to bear and survive the competition. The world is very tough and performing takes a lot of courage. People with prominent cheeks have been instrumental in all the major battles, wars, and conflicts in the world.

2. Prominent Cheeks Angled Down, Slanting below the Nose (Middling Cheeks)

People who have prominent cheekbones but possess cheeks that are below the nose have the same leadership qualities as those with prominent cheeks, however these people are not as domineering and authoritative as people with prominent cheeks. They are very adventurous and bold. They also love to travel and are full of life. These people are also very sexual and their sexuality increases if they have dimples on their cheeks. They are more refined then the previous category of people in terms of style, elegance, language, and behaviour. They love life and desire friends, family, and excitement, that's the reason this region is also called the 'Breath of life'. The fuller this area of the face, the more vivacious, charming, and lively, the person is.

3. Hollowed/Sunken Middle Cheeks

If the middle cheeks of a person become hollow and start sinking deep inside, then the person is said to have lost his/her desire for life. These people sink deep into despondency because of the negativity within them. They are basically negative thinkers, as we generally find that those who have reached the last stage of their lives, or those who are very unwell and are in hospital for a long time, have such cheeks.

When we see such cheeks we should conclude that the person has struggled a lot in his/her life and because of fate, dwindling income, and constant failure in life, this person has become very depressed and hopeless and has lost his/her desire to struggle and advance in life. If the other features on the face are also negative, then these people will have suicidal tendencies. You will generally find that those who are chain smokers, drug addicts, have such cheeks and they are very faint-hearted. These people do not have the courage to face life and to struggle for survival. Hence, they generally adopt measures that slowly destroy them.

4. Prominent Cheekbones with Sunken Cheeks

If the cheekbones are high and prominent, but the cheeks are sunken then this indicates contradictory elements in the person's personality. These people might also have lost their will-power to reach a supreme position in life, or even if they have the will-power then also they might be looking out for shortcuts to fulfil their desires.

5. Narrow (Sunken) but Strong Cheekbones

This is an extended version of the previous kind of cheekbones. If the prominent cheekbones are sunken, but strong and distinct, then these people will have the same qualities as that of the people in the previous category, however these people will also be very stubborn, adamant, and difficult to deal with.

Because of their stubborn and adamant nature, even those who love them very much are not able to live with them in the long run. The ruling planet for prominent cheekbones is Mars, and if there is even the slightest fault in the position of Mars, it becomes self-destructive for the person concerned. So, the proper advice of a bona fide spiritual master should be taken in cases where a person is badly affected by the negative presence of Mars in his/her natal chart.

6. Wide Cheekbones

People with wide cheek-bones are very proud and driven. Generally, people who have wide cheekbones are blessed to have authority. These people will make extremely good leaders. Such cheeks are common in squarish faces. However if the cheekbones are wide and placed high, then these people fall in the category of high and wide cheekbones. People whose cheekbones are generally high and wide are so proud, authoritative, and domina-ting that it becomes difficult for others to adjust with them. If you have such cheekbones, then make sure you do not stretch or exaggerate your dominating and bossy nature, especially if you are a woman, as prominent cheekbones are not considered good for women.

7. Angular, Sharp or Pointed Cheekbones

If the cheekbones are angular, sharp or pointed, then the cheeks are not too fleshy. Those who have prominent cheeks, protruding out of their face distinctly, have such cheeks. People with these cheeks are very economical, frugal, and thrifty. They will not like to spend money upon expensive things and will always go to several different shops to find the cheapest option. Even if these people are buying a pair of jeans, they won't be interested in the brand. They will just check that the clothes they are buying are economical and the cheapest.

8. Flat Cheeks or Cheekbones

As the name itself suggests, these cheeks will not be prominent at all, neither in the middle, nor above the nose. These people disdain and resist authority, and do not like telling people what should be done and how it should be done. They believe in complete freedom of expression. As they do not like to give orders, likewise they do not like to be told what should be done, and what should not be done.

CATEGORISATION OF CHEEKBONES ACCORDING TO THEIR SETTING

1. Cheekbones set closer to the Nose

People with cheekbones set closer to their nose are also very authoritative; however these people will generally give others enough time to follow their orders. Even if these people have to punish others, they are more likely to have given a warning before the final ultimatum. They possess all the qualities of people with prominent cheeks, however are more considerate when it comes to dealing with others.

2. Cheekbones set closer to the Ears

People whose cheekbones are set closer to the ears are stronger, and make strict bosses. Once these people give an order they are unlikely to wait for you to execute it, as they expect others to act quickly and comply with their orders and authority. People with such cheekbones are very proud, dominant, authoritative, and stubborn. They are so adamant and stubborn that they will rarely budge from their position, once they have taken a stance and are more likely to get into confrontations.

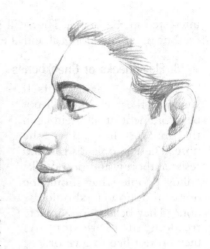

SOME OF THE VERY IMPORTANT FEATURES OF THE CHEEKS

1. Full Fleshy Cheeks

Those who are very sensual have full, fleshy cheeks. Apart from their sensuality, these people are also very confident,

vivacious, and practical, and want to enjoy their lives to the fullest. They love sex and food, and need lots of quality food and sex for their survival. Their practicality can be ascertained from the fact that they need the best rewards and turnovers for whatever they start. They will also not fall in love blindly, but will prefer to ascertain every facet of their spouse, before getting married. Sometimes, these people are considered to be very lazy. They might procrastinate, and also tend to work very slowly.

2. Round Upper Cheeks/ Apple Cheeks

People with round upper cheeks are among those who are not very homely. These people are also very strong willed and have an immense amount of confidence within them. They are generous and courageous as well, so they are the ideal choice for business endeavours. You will find many people at the very top of corporate hierarchies with such cheeks.

3. Fleshy Round Cheeks

People with full round cheeks have a chubbier look on their face because of lots of fat in their cheeks. These people are generally ruled by the water element and are very emotional. Full round cheeks also indicate that the person is very sensual.

4. Wrinkled, Thin Sagging Cheeks

People with lots of wrinkles on their cheeks, which seem lifeless and sagged, suffer a lot in life. Their financial conditions are not good and they need to work very hard to earn money.

They always think about how they will be able to make arrangements for tomorrow, what the future of their children and family would be, and what they should do to increase their savings, etc.

5. Dimples on the Cheeks

People with dimples on their cheeks, are avid attention seekers. These people like getting pampered all the time and they might also have lots of admirers surrounding them. They are also pampered at home, so because of this they might become very fickle and are constantly prone to mood swings. However, not everyone with dimples are fickle-minded.

Dimples on the cheeks also indicate that the person can be authoritative. So, it should be noted that dimples on the cheeks also represent influence, authority, and wealth. These dimples also indicate an extremely sexual nature.

6. Red or Pink Cheeks

Red or pink cheeks have the same significance as red or pink lips. Naturally red cheeks, like the red lips, indicate good health and vitality of a person. It should also be noted that cheeks become naturally red even when a person blushes.

CHAPTER 13
. . . .
JAWS

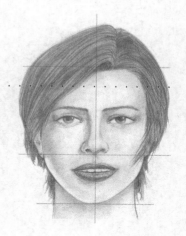

The face is basically the map of our life's journey which contains everything like the lines, mounts, etc., and jaws are the major indicators in our face which helps us determine our attitudes, principles, ethics, choices, how rooted we are to our beliefs and the way we handle conflicts. So, this is a highly significant part of our face and is the only fascinating bony structure in the face that comes naturally with its own built-in hinge. Reading the jaw is slightly different from reading other facial features like the eyes, noses, mouths etc., because the eyes, noses, mouths come in different shapes, sizes and features, however while reading the jaws we have to concentrate mostly upon the overall structure and the built-in pattern. Jaws are ruled by Mars in Vedic physiognomy and basically control the age patterns from 58 onwards and have an impact upon a few selective years in the age group of eighties as well as nineties.

Jaws can basically be categorised upon the basis of their width, prominence, and evenness. Now let's discuss in detail about the different categories of jaws and their significance.

CATEGORISATION OF JAWS ACCORDING TO THEIR WIDTH

1. Wide Jaw

What is the parameter with which we determine wide jaws? Wide jaws basically have nothing to do with how fleshy or bony

your face looks. Wideness of the jaw can be calculated only upon the basis of how wide the lower part of the face is. Some people have a very wide upper part because of their wide forehead, but the width decreases towards the chin and the facial structure becomes narrow. Some people have very wide lower structures of the face because of their wide jaw, however the width decreases towards the forehead because these people have narrow foreheads. However, there are others as well who have both very wide upper and lower parts. A wide upper part because of their wide foreheads and wide lower part because of their wide jaw.

The easiest way to determine a wide jaw is just by taking a look at face and seeing which part of the face is broad. Are both the upper and the lower parts broad? Is the lower part broader than the upper part? Are you able to clearly see the side parts of the face below the ears i.e. the jaws, while looking at the face? If the answer to any of these two questions is yes, then the person you are assessing, possesses a broad jaw.

Now just look at the forehead and compare the width of the jaw with the forehead, as it is extremely important to determine which of the two is boarder. Now while comparing the width of the jaw with the forehead width, what do you notice? You will definitely notice one of three things. Firstly, either the forehead is broader than the jaw. Secondly, both the forehead and the jaw might be equal in width. Thirdly, the jaw is greater in width than the forehead because the forehead is narrower. In the above mentioned three categories wide jaws are those that fall in the second and the third category. Now you have understood what I wanted you to and now you will have to pause and read between the lines to ascertain the meaning of wide jaws in Vedic physiognomy.

Wide jaws are the representative of masculinity and dominance, which are basic requirements in aggressive professions like defence, sports like martial arts, boxing, football etc. Now I believe that you can easily understand that wide jaws could easily result in aggressiveness. Now let us discuss both the cases of wide jaws:

a. Jaw equals the forehead in width:

If the proportion of width of the jaw is equal to the forehead width then this person might not be into any aggressive professions but is mentally very aggres-sive. Once these people take a firm stand, they are not going to bow down as they are strong decision makers. These people play mental games of power and might not get physically or emotionally involved in anything.

b. Jaw width greater than the forehead width:

In this case you will notice that the face of the person broadens as you go down and the upper part of the face is narrow. Now when the forehead is narrow and the jaw is broad, just think what will it mean? Remember we divided the face into three horizontal sections according to the three modes of the material nature in the beginning of this book, in the section division of the face. In that section the face was divided into the modes of goodness, passion and ignorance. Now just imagine the mode of goodness being narrower or both the mode of goodness and passion being narrower and the mode of ignorance being broader.

This will clearly mean that these people work in the mode of ignorance and do not have any reasoning, whatsoever. They will just be physically so aggressive that they might tend to force their opinions upon others and if others do not follow their opinions, they might become violent and might make the use of force or power to make others understand and follow their beliefs.

2. Average Jaw

An average jaw is a jaw which is slightly less than the forehead in width, however it is not too narrow. The easiest way to distinguish narrow jaws and average jaws are by remembering that narrow jaws look like a 'V' in the lower part of the face, but in average jaws, the jaw is slightly lesser in width than the forehead and the shape of the face is not like a downward angled triangle.

Average jawed people do not get into conflicts immediately, unlike the wide jawed people. This means that an average jawed person might be better in identifying the problems related to the conflict, i.e. forecasting it beforehand and resolving the cause of the conflict and getting out of it as soon as possible. Average jawed ones might make their own paths and excel in their fields of interest without getting involved in cut-throat competition.

3. Narrow Jaw

People with narrow jaws are quite giving and considerate when it comes to functioning in this world. These people will always avoid getting into arguments as they are not very aggressive.

Again the faiths and beliefs of these people are not as strong as of those with wide jaws. These people tend to get swayed away by the beliefs and thoughts of others and it is very easy for show-offs to impress them. They also tend to be fickle minded and hence might procrastinate their work schedules for the sake of pleasure, friends, or other things.

These people also might be very timid and hence might lack the spirit to face challenges and might believe that whatever comes to them without any effort is good enough for their survival. Men with lower parts (especially their jaws) narrower than their foreheads are most often ruled by women in their personal and professional lives.

CATEGORISATION OF THE JAWS ACCORDING TO THE BONE FORMATTING

1. Very Bony Jaw

In some people, the bone of the jaw is very clearly seen jutting out, this can be seen from the front or the back of their face. People with such jaws are extremely driven. They are just intoxicated by money, glamour and power and nothing seems fruitful enough to them as compared to material things. These people are so madly driven that they become ruthless and careless about who and what is in their way. They will not mind trampling others under their feet for their own gain, even if those people are their own friends or families, as they do not care for others at all.

Vedic physiognomy is of the opinion that women with very bony jaws (or wide jaws) are extremely unfortunate for others. These women can put their spouses and employers in trouble at any time.

2. Protruding Jaw

This jaw is the mother of bony jaws. The jaws are so bony that they tend to stick out from the face. These jaws sometimes seem as if they will tear the skin to land out in open. Just walk behind the person, and then walk past them at any angle and you will very clearly be able to see these jaws. Just like their jaws are screaming to be free from the skin, likewise their characters and personalities want to be freed too. These people tend to behave in an outrageous manner, as if they are screaming to fulfil their own selfish motives and desires by hook or crook. They take others, including their own families as sacrificial lambs and will sacrifice all relationships for their own selfish motives. Be cautious while dealing with women with such jaws (very bony/protruding/wide jaws) as these jaws are not considered to be fortunate for women.

3. Uneven Jaw

Uneven jaws are those that are not even on the left and the right sides of the face. These jaws will have a different shape, size or structure on the left and the right sides. One side of the jaw might be pointed or protruding while the other side might be recessed. In any case, the proportion of the jaws will be uneven on the left and the right sides of the face.

People with uneven jaws tend to possess uneven temperaments. These people will work in extremes, so you will notice extreme reactions from them. Protruding jaws can also be taken as uneven jaws because in spite of the jaws being similar on both the sides, these jaws do not have an even surface and are like two bumps on the face which could be compared to bumps on the road.

4. Even Jaws

Even jaws are those jaws which have an even surface and are symmetrical on both sides of the face. These jaws are neither bony nor protruding and are ideal among all jaw types. Generally the growth of a person's face stabilises by the age of 21. So after this age the jawbones should not be overtly exposed or pointed and should be even. The jaw bones should also be symmetrical and should be very beautifully formed on the face.

People possessing even jaws are even minded and never work in extremes. These people will not get involved in any kind of strife uselessly and if any kind of strife takes place, then also they generally find conciliatory methods to end that strife. They tend to follow the middle path and are always very considerate and sensitive about other people's issues as well. Also, people with even jaws are not very aggressive and tread very softly in each and every situation and endeavour.

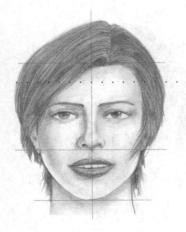

CHIN

Army personnel, soldiers, and those in military schools are taught to stand straight, thrust their chests forward, keep their head straight, and push the chin up. 'Taking it on the chin' means you won't back down. And a famous proverb indicates, 'If you are distressed, or feel down, all you need to do is keep your chin up and all will be well'.

The chin has a very important place in face reading. It signifies dominance, strength, character, and the person's will. Will here refers to will-power, tenaciousness, and the willingness of a person to lead his life on his own terms. However, it should be noted that the chin specifically deals with dominance.

Generally, people are not able to follow the voice in their heart because of some kind of fear. Only very few people are strong-willed and courageous enough to dare to listen to their heart, and make their dreams come true. Such strong heartedness or faint heartedness can be easily ascertained just by looking at the chin.

The Vedic texts are of the opinion that will-power is necessary for the formation of character, character is necessary for discipline, discipline is necessary for moral conduct, and moral conduct is necessary for self-realisation. Vedic texts have glorified character and moral conduct, stating that people who are able to develop and build these two pious traits within themselves are rewarded with life on their own terms. Don't confuse character and morality with stubbornness, as most people tend to be very stubborn and foolishly conclude that they are people of character and high moral values. A proverb states, 'You need guts to have glory', and how much guts a person has can be easily determined by the chin. The chin represents how life will be during the seventies. Chins can be broadly classified into several types, based on length, breadth, thrust, curve etc.

CATEGORISATION OF CHIN ACCORDING TO WIDTH

1. Broad Chin

People with a broad chin are very strong-willed, confident, ambitious, aggressive, and enterprising. These people follow strict rules and are very ethical if they run a business. However, such a chin is not considered very good for those looking for romantic relationships. These people like to be very honest and dedicated, and

focus completely on business, and hardly pay attention to their love life. This makes their partners feel choked in the relationship.

2. Extremely Broad Chin

People with extremely broad chins are most often tyrants, as these people possess zero tolerance towards others, especially if those people are disobedient. Again, these people will be very harmful if they also have tightly-pursed lips. They will definitely harm others, if they can, and have the power to harm others even if the offence is small.

3. Narrow Chin

A narrow chin represents less energy and drive. These people do not completely utilise their mental and physical strength. Hence, most people with narrow chins are not able to gain what they want in their lives, and live a very mediocre life. These people are also very sensitive, delicate and uncertain. People with narrow chins tend to falter and get carried away by the ideologies and thoughts of others. They cannot make their own stand.

CATEGORISATION OF CHIN ACCORDING TO ITS LENGTH

1. Long Chin

People with long chins are very warm, friendly, and affectionate. Most of these people also possess a good sense of humour. Long chins also represent that the person is very organised and is highly energetic and adventurous. These people are involved in adventurous activities and will participate in sports and play by the rules. Also these people are very interested in sex. So, they tend to be unusually

biased towards those who give them sexual favours. Hence, people with long chins are not faithful and reliable as far as matters of fidelity are concerned. It should also be noted that if the chin is unusually long, then these people fall into the mode of ignorance.

2. Short/Small Chin

The greatest challenge for short chinned people is to be strong, and develop strong will-power. So, since small chins are considered to be weak, the advice to people with a small chin is that they should behave cautiously and try not to be overshadowed by negative circumstances.

3. Very Small Chin

People with a very small chin will certainly find it difficult to live life on their own terms and to cope with negative situations and challenges. These people get scared very easily, feel demoralised, and suppressed by negative circumstances in their life and by those who possess

more dominating facial traits. It should be noted that as Mars rules the chin, so a weaker chin indicates the feeble position of Mars in the natal chart. So, the challenge for people with a very small chin (or those with weaker facial features) is to find the strength to face challenges and lead their own life. These people need to get out of the habit of saying, 'I can't do this', 'I can't do that, it is beyond my strength', 'I am helpless', etc. Such people tend to perceive advice, or any disagreement as criticism. So these people should definitely try to increase their potential and discover their creativity. They should pay attention to the advice they receive and not misconstrue what well-meaning people tell them.

CATEGORISATION OF CHIN ACCORDING TO THE CHIN THRUST

1. Jutting Chin

Jutting chins extend outwards. As a fledgling face reader, if you are confused while determining whether the chin is jutting, or receding, then you can draw an imaginary line starting from the forehead, coming down to the chin. Check whether the angle of the chin is straight, in-turned, or out-turned.

If the chin looks out-turned, or out-angled, then the person has a lot of chin thrust and is said to possess a jutting chin. Out-angled chins are related to competitiveness. These people are generally very disobedient and openly resist things that are not as per their own beliefs. They will act as per their own fancy and will have a flagrant disregard for the advice of parents, or any other authority above them.

People with jutting chins are very strong-willed. They tend to digest whatever they eat. Most of these people do not generally have a regulated balanced diet, so they might stay lean and thin, or might be unusually healthy. You will rarely find obese people in this category.

2. Receding Chin

Receding chins are those that are inward angled, towards the throat. A receding chin is called a weak chin which represents the

complete opposite behaviour and traits of those with a chin that juts out. These people lack confidence and tend to get scared very easily by any kind of competition. Most of them are also frightened of speaking in public, groups, or with people of the opposite sex. Most of these people have an innate stage fright so they think they are very incompetent when it comes to giving any public speech or presentation. These people have an innate urge to gain the respect of others and need a lot of 'buttering' and appreciation. This attitude results in stubborn behaviour. So the main challenge for these people is to control their expectation of unnecessary adulation, and to overcome their childlike attitude of stubbornness, and behave in a much more mature way.

3. Even/Straight Chin

Even chins are neither inward angled nor outward angled. People with straight chins are the most ideal among all the three categories. People with straight chins do not show unnecessary emotions and are very suave, articulate, and determined. They are also very straightforward in their approach towards life and mostly possess balanced personalities. Even if these people compete with others, they won't allow the competitiveness to come to

the surface, unless they possess very broad jaws, protruding cheekbones, or some other feature on their face which portrays excessive aggressiveness.

DIFFERENT TYPES OF CHINS

1. Pointed Chin

Pointed chins are those that have a triangular end. People with pointed chins cannot stay alone as they have a great urge to make friends and to get everyone's attention. These people are also greatly driven by lust, and are ruled by their emotions. So, they may not be satisfied by any single object or relationship. They are prone to mood swings within short intervals. These people are also very impatient and tend to make quick decisions.

2. Square Chin

These chins have a squarish outline. People with square chins are very demanding in love and personal relation-ships. These people are humourless and have a difficult character. Square chins also reveal stubbornness.

People with square chins are also very combative and defensive, so it becomes very difficult for square chinned people to acknowledge their own mistakes and faults. These

people also have the tendency of finding faults in others. They are also very moody and impatient. They do not have the patience to wait for a long time, and if their patience is tested, they might become abusive and violent.

3. Round Chin

People with round chins are very generous, courteous, and family-oriented. These people are also very good listeners and good at giving advice.

4. Fleshy Chin

Fleshy chins are those that have an extra padding on the chin, because of the fleshy tissue within the chin. Any unnecessary amount of fleshy tissue, or padding on the chin, signifies stubbornness. Stubbornness becomes more prominent if these chins jut out as well. These people possess a very annoying working style, and aren't very tolerant or even-tempered.

If these people also have protruding or wide jaws, and prominent cheeks or cheekbones, then they will definitely be tyrants, such as Saddam Hussein.

5. Turned Up Chin

If the end of the chin turns up so as to make a horizontal line

or cleft on the chin, then these people are also very stubborn and will represent the same characteristics and traits as those with a fleshy chin. So, whether the chin is fleshy, upturned, or has a horizontal line, or cleft, in between the mouth and the chin (which mostly happens because the chin is upturned) all these three kinds of people will portray stubbornness and have an adamant nature.

CATEGORISATION OF THE CHIN ACCORDING TO DIFFERENT FEATURES

1. Dimples on the Chin

People with dimples on the chin are very sexual and flirtatious. They have strong sexual appetites and possess heightened emotions. They are also attention seekers and enjoy flirting just because they need people to give them all the attention they need. Also, as their emotions are heightened, so they get sexually aroused very quickly. They might also start laughing or crying very easily in the course of events, or during a conversation.

2. Cleft between the Chin

Generally, it is observed that some people have a cleft in the middle of their chin. A cleft in the middle of the chin represents a deeply promiscuous nature. So people with a cleft on their chin are definitely very sexual and would like to have many sexual partners. It should be noted that the chin is ruled by the water element, so clefts on the chin are also indicative of the fear of drowning.

As it has already been explained in previous chapters, the face is horizontally divided into three sections based on the modes of material natures, so it should be noted here that even though some of the chin types might be considered stronger than the others, because of their being long, broad, etc., even then a longer lower section, i.e. the section from the nose to the chin, means that the person is in the mode of ignorance.

BEARD AND MOUSTACHE

THE BEARD

The beard is one of the important indicators of personality and character. It is also considered to be a tool used to hide many personality traits. While observing the beard and the moustache, the main things to be observed are the direction of the hair growth, how dense the beard is, and its colour.

1. The Auspicious Beard

Auspicious beards are those that are not too thick and dense. These beards will not have heavy bushy hair growth, and the hair will grow below the nose, only on the lower part of the cheeks, around the jaw line, and the chin. When these beards are joined with a moustache, they should form a W-shaped curve around the mouth. In such beards, the hairline of the beard is such that small patches of skin are revealed on both sides of the lower lip and a thin section of the beard joins the middle part of the lower lip, giving a W-shape to the beard. The beard should also be even with soft, fine, and shiny hair, i.e. the beard should not be coarse, rough, dry, very thick, or uneven. If the beard grows in such a fashion, then it is the most auspicious among all kinds of beards on the human face. Such a beard is an indication of royalty, courage, strength, wisdom, self-control, compassion, asceticism and a cheerful spirit.

2. Thick Beard Covering the Chin

If the beard of the person grows in such a manner that it is very thick and bushy and it covers the whole chin as well as the cheeks and does not even leave patches of hair on both sides of the lower lip, then such a beard represents a highly sexual person. These people are also rough, wild, and impetuous.

3. Wiry and Coarse Beard

Beards that are wiry and coarse represent mean-spirited people. People with such a beard think they are very noble and are connoisseurs of knowledge; however all their actions are only directed towards the fulfilment of their personal motives.

4. Thin, Patchy Beard

In cases where the beard growth is thin and patchy, or where the growth of the beard is like coarse wiry patches of hair, then these people tend to possess weak constitutions. Most of these

people might also be short, or might have a very slender or fragile
frame.

NATURE AND CHARACTER OF MATERIALISTS SPORTING A HEAVY BEARD

If a person is working on a materialistic plane, and still
permanently sports a heavy beard, then it should definitely be
considered that this person wants to hide his immaturity and
inferiority complex, by looking more mature and masculine in
front of people. These people actually want others to fear and
respect them. They also possess very secretive dispositions, i.e. if
they know something which could benefit others, they will
definitely not tell those people about it, and would like to receive
the full benefit themselves. Another important thing to be noted
is that if any person working in this material world who is actively
involved in materialistic activities, purposely sports a beard, then
such a person also possesses a jealous and very possessive nature.
For example, these men get extremely jealous if they see someone
else enjoying the company of women. Most wars, fights, and
scuffles that these men get involved into, are usually related to
women. These people are very adamant, aggressive, and barbaric.

NATURE AND CHARACTER OF TRANSCENDENTALISTS SPORTING A HEAVY BEARD

If a person is a transcendentalist then the beard is a sign of
fulfilment, peace, renunciation, penance, truth, knowledge, and
compassion. Transcendentalists do not usually cut their hair, or
beard, so they also have long, matted locks apart from the long
beard. If, however, a person is not a transcendentalist and is
involved in material activities, then the person falls into the
category of materialists sporting heavy beard.

COLOUR OF THE BEARD

The best colour of a beard that is long is black. Black gives the
person an attractive personality. If a person has an auspicious
beard and its colour is black then he will definitely possess a

hypnotic and attractive personality. If, however, the beard is of some colour other than black, then the categorisation of hair according to different colours and textures, should be referred to in the chapter on hair.

MOUSTACHE

In ancient times, moustaches were considered to be the sign of masculinity. Today also, people who wish to look very masculine and mature definitely sport a beard and a moustache. Beard and moustaches aren't separately read, they are read together. So, the conditions that are applicable for an auspicious beard will also be applicable for an auspicious moustache. However, it should be noted that there should be no bald patch on the philtrum because if the moustache does not grow on the philtrum and there is a patch there, then the person will become the subject of slander and criticism wherever he goes. The situation of this person will worsen with age.

Finally, it should be noted that a beard, or moustache, on a woman's face is considered to be highly inauspicious. Generally, a beard or moustache appears on a woman's face because of hormonal imbalance; however this indicates a lot of suffering in life. These women will have a rocky adult life, and difficult old age. It should also be noted that even if the lady does not have a beard or moustache but only a thin line of hair in the beard or moustache area, even then they will fall in this category. Women with a thin line of hair in the moustache area, or women with hair on the chin, have loose morals, are untrustworthy, and unpredictable.

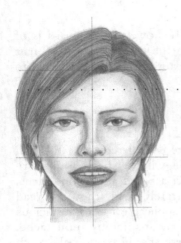

NECK AND THROAT

THE NECK

The neck is not exactly a part of the face, but is definitely part of the head. The head starts above the shoulders, which includes the neck as well. As this book is related to face reading, so I will give just an overview of the significance of the neck in face reading. While reading the face, a few features of the neck should be kept in mind, which play a vital role in assessing the exact nature, character, destiny, and consciousness of a person. Firstly, the height and thickness of the neck should be considered. Secondly, moles, dents, and birthmarks on the neck should also be properly analysed.

CATEGORISATION OF NECK ACCORDING TO ITS LENGTH

1. Long Neck

The length of the neck is particularly important in determining the exact consciousness and behavioural pattern of a person. In face reading, we can generally make out the mindset and the constitution of a person by looking at the neck. A long neck refers to the normal, or ideal length of the neck. These people are generally open-hearted and accepting in terms of new ideas, concepts, and ideologies. They are also very confident about whatever they do, and do not possess a fault-finding attitude (if other inauspicious features are not present on their face). A long neck is also associated with good intelligence and forecasting skills. These people are full of life, spirit, and vivaciousness. A long neck is considered to be a symbol of beauty, especially in women.

However, extraordinarily long necks indicate a faulty natal chart. These people are deprived of wealth and reason, and live a life of bondage and slavery.

2. Short and Stocky Neck

People with a short and stocky neck (especially women) suffer from an inferiority complex. These people (especially women) are bereft of energy, beauty and virtue, and hence their performance level is also nearly zero, and therefore they are generally in the throes of hatred, jealousy. They have a domineering and adamant nature. These women are generally jealous of those women who are very beautiful, hardworking, and virtuous. Hence, most of these women generally adopt a fault-finding and sarcastic nature. If a woman has a very short neck, it indicates childlessness.

3. Mediocre Neck

Mediocre necks are those that are neither long, nor too short, but of medium length. People with mediocre length necks are neither too open, nor too closed, in terms of their nature and behaviour. These people are neither too divine or heavenly in their temperament, nor are they deeply buried in hedonistic, or material things. Most people with such a neck take a lot of time to think about what should be done, or what should not be done, as their minds are not as sharp as those who have a long neck. These people do not act impulsively like those with a short neck.

CATEGORISATION OF NECK ACCORDING TO ITS THICKNESS

1. Thin and Fragile Neck

Necks that are thin and fragile often represent lack of life's forces. These people lack stamina, power, and resilience. Most such people also have fragile bodies. Thin and fragile necks represent a weak constitution. Most of these people easily fall prey to sickness and diseases. Problems related to lungs and breathing is common with them. Since these people lack stamina and resilience, if they ever start facing bad times then it becomes difficult for them to get back to their normal position, unless they have some strong support. As these people lack physical strength so they should mostly try to develop themselves intellectually and spiritually, to rise in life.

2. Even and Strong Neck

A strong and sturdy neck that is evenly built and is neither too thick nor thin is representative of resilience, power, and stamina.

3. Thick Neck

Necks that are too thick are not considered to be very good in terms of one's thoughts, behaviour, and constitution. As already discussed about a short and stocky neck, people with a thick neck are libidinous and hedonistic, and have a slothful approach towards life.

Women with fat and wide necks are bereft of all virtues. These women are very ill-mannered, mischievous, faulty, immoral and wicked. Very fleshy, fat, and thick necks are also a sign of widowhood in women. These people live unhappy lives.

THROAT

The throat is ruled by the planet Venus. While assessing the throat, it should be determined if the throat is recessed, or protruding. Any moles, dents, lines, and birthmarks on the throat should also be properly analysed.

CATEGORISATION OF THE THROAT ACCORDING TO ITS FULLNESS

1. Full Throat

Fullness of the throat is always judged by looking at the Adam's Apple and the vocal chords. If the Adam's Apple has some elevation then the throat is considered to be full, and if the Adam's Apple or vocal chords seem to be recessed, then the throat is said to be recessed. Throats that are full with certain elevation of the Adam's Apple are considered to be the best among all. Full throats produce strong vibrations of power and authority, and if a person possesses long, broad, or double Fa Ling lines and if there is single vertical line in the third eye region then full throats will help increment the power and authority the person has.

2. Recessed Throats

As full throats are considered to produce vibrations of power and authority, likewise recessed throats become instrumental in checking and restricting that power and authority. So, even if a person possess broad, long, or double Fa Ling lines, but if the nose and the throat are flat, or recessed, then the person's power and authority ceases and that power is passed to the progeny. So these people are also deprived of wealth. However, if a person possesses superior features indicating power, like the vertical line exactly in the third eye region or the 'divine chakra' in the central axis, then the build of the throat might have a negligible effect upon power and authority. However, it should be noted that people with a 'divine chakra' or vertical line in the third eye region are always full throated. As already mentioned, people generally get things in packages, so features on the face and features on the other parts of the body will always coincide and correspond with each other instead of contradicting each other.

3. Protruding Throat (Protruding Adam's Apple)

There are some people whose neck is not even long and strong, but they still possess a protruding Adam's Apple. People whose Adam's Apple sticks out from their throats, and protrudes in an unnecessary fashion show excessive behaviour when it comes to some things that they like. These people are highly materialistic and desire an excess in things concerned with sex, money, or other material pleasures, depending upon their individual tastes and likes.

VISIBILITY OF FOLDS ON THE THROAT

Three Visible Folds on the Throat

If three visible folds of the vocal chords appear on the throat then they are generally considered auspicious. Three visible folds generally indicate that the person concerned will live a life of comfort and pleasure because of the auspicious placement of Venus in the natal chart and he/she will not have to struggle a lot for wealth. Most of these people (especially women) will possess extreme good luck if other features on their faces are also auspicious. Women in this category might get married into a wealthy family, or someone possessing a lot of wealth might favour them a lot. For men, the three visible folds on the vocal chord indicate a position of name, fame, power, and money. As full vocal chords produce strong vibrations for power and authority, so men with three visible folds are generally endowed with astounding luck and authority. Again, as the throat in the body is linked to speech, so these people will generally be able to control the masses through their influential words. These people are very suave, articulate, and dexterous. They are also very refined, polished and stylish. People get greatly influenced and motivated by their personality. So there are strong vibrations of good luck and authority in these people's natal charts.

HORIZONTAL LINES AND MOUNTS
OF THE FOREHEAD

PART III

Lines

HORIZONTAL LINES AND MOUNTS ON THE FOREHEAD

As discussed earlier, the forehead is divided horizontally into three different zones, i.e. observation, memory, and imagination zones. So, let's discuss in detail how the three zones can affect the destiny of a person.

RIGHT

LEFT

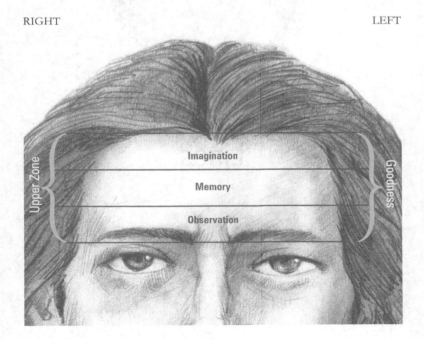

CHAPTER 1
HORIZONTAL LINES AND MOUNTS ON THE FOREHEAD

1. Zone one, the Observation Zone

According to Vedic face readers, this zone is referred to as the instinctual zone of the face, since it gives information about the person's basic instincts. If this zone is powerful then the essential foundation, or the fundamental structure of the person, is said to be very powerful. This zone is ruled by three major planets — Venus, Sun, and Mars. The planet Venus rules the area just above the left eyebrow in Men and right eyebrow in Women, and the Sun rules the area just above the right eyebrow in Men and left eyebrow in Women. Mars is situated above the Sun and Venus. Now, let us discuss in detail the importance of these planets on the forehead.

a. The Mount of Venus

The Mount of Venus represents the Indian God Kama who is also known as the God of love, desire, and creativity. Kama is one of the prominent demigods in Vedic scriptures, and is related to creativity, good fortune, money, luxury, and abundant wealth. It should be noted that the planet Venus is typically known as Shukra in Hindu mythology and is the son of the great seer Bhrigu. *Shukra* in Sanskrit means 'semen'. So, Shukra is a Brahmin who is an embodiment of love and represents refined taste romance, beauty, sensuality, wealth, comforts, luxuries, jewellery, arts, etc. Among all the seasons, Shukra represents spring. Silver is

RIGHT   LEFT

Line of Moon
Line of Saturn
Line of Jupiter
Line of Mercury
Line of Mars
Line of Sun
                                                            Line of Venus

the metal of Venus; its gemstone is diamond; its day is Friday. Venus rules the number six in Indian numerology.

If this part of the forehead is clear without any moles, or inauspicious marks, and is moderately developed and shiny then this is a good omen which indicates that the person will earn money and live a luxurious life. People with a well-developed Mount of Venus are generally successful artists, writers, singers, music directors, composers, filmmakers, and producers. People with extraordinary artistic calibre will have a horizontal line on the mount of Venus, called the Line of Venus. This Line is exactly above the left eyebrow, on the Mount of Venus, which increases the functional effect of the Mount of Venus. Without the Line of Venus, the Mount of Venus has a diminished effect, or sometimes no effect.

Shukra, or Venus, is also important because of its association with the science of mantras, Arurvedic medicine, tantra, the casting of spells, hypnotism, mesmerism, and alchemy.

As the Mount of Venus and the Line of Venus represent good

fortune, luck, and wealth; an excessively developed Mount of Venus indicates bad fortune, loss of creativity, and evil thoughts. If a person has a highly protruding Mount of Venus, this means it is over-developed and that the person will have highly protruding brow bones, or two or three Lines of Venus, or both. These people are generally criminals and rapists with excessive sexual appetites and an excessive desire for enjoyment, wealth, and power. Women with an excessively developed Mount of Venus are generally nymphomaniacs. These women are excessively greedy as well, so they madly desire sex and money. They generally earn money by selling their bodies and are involved in the flesh trade. People with an excessively developed Mount of Venus with two or more lines on it, fall in the mode of ignorance and might have an animalistic approach towards life.

b. The Mount of Sun

Sun is known as *Surya* in Sanskrit. The Mount of Sun represents the Sun God, which represents glory, fame, power, administrative abilities, and wealth. The Mount of Sun is just above the right eyebrows, and if this part is evenly developed and shiny then this indicates the presence of the Mount of Sun. As

RIGHT   LEFT

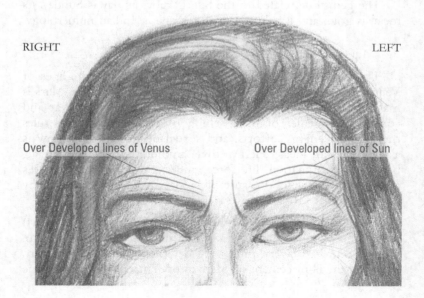

Over Developed lines of Venus   Over Developed lines of Sun

the Sun is representative of the fire element, this entire area is governed by the fire element. The fiery nature represents intellectual capabilities and provides flight to a person's thoughts. Great celebrities, politicians, leaders, and people who live in high society generally have the Mount of Sun. The presence of the Mount of Sun, like the Mount of Venus, is felt by the presence of a horizontal line, called the Line of Sun. People with the auspicious presence of the Line of Sun will remain famous throughout their lives, irrespective of the career or profession they belong to.

If the Mount of Sun represents glory, fame, wealth, and popularity then an overdeveloped Mount of Sun with more than one line, i.e. two, three, or more lines, indicates a tyrant. People in this category are madly inclined towards attaining glory, power and position by using any means, without giving any consideration to ethics, and morality. These people will display a highly aggressive, dominating, and controlling nature. They possess zero tolerance for anything that goes against their nature, or thoughts, and become very rigid and inflexible in their ideologies, and thoughts. As the Sun works against these people, so they will also be defamed and lose their reputation in life.

The gemstone related to the Sun is ruby; its day is Sunday, its metal is gold; and it rules the number one in Indian numerology.

c. Line of Mars

The Line of Mars on the forehead is just above the lines of Venus and the Sun. Mars is known as *Mangala* in Sanskrit. Mars is masculine, hot, and a fiery planet. He is the God of War and commander-in-chief of the assembly of nine planets. Mars rules the physical energy, efforts, and sexual desires. Its red glow is associated with ideas, energy, drive, ambition, strength, courage, bravery, determination, life force, and expansion. Mars signifies administrative abilities. Because of its fiery nature, people ruled by Mars will most probably have a squarish face.

The absence of Mars on the forehead (or in the natal chart) makes the people dreamers, lazy, and devoid of health, wealth, virility, courage, bravery, prosperity, determination, and versatility. However the ill-placement of Mars in one's natal chart makes one adamant, fickle-minded, unethical, quarrelsome, violent, cruel, afflicted in body and mind as well as devoid of wealth, longevity, and education. So, only the auspicious placement of Mars endows people with health, wealth, prosperity, virility, fame, power, and a regal status. In case of the auspicious placement of Mars, the person will also be full of life, adventurous, enthusiastic, articulate, and determined.

The word 'martial' is derived from 'Mars', hence people in defence, martial arts, police and administration possess Mars in exalted positions in their natal charts.

Mars rules number nine in Indian numerology; its metal is iron; its day is Tuesday; and its gemstone is red coral.

2. Zone Two, the Memory Zone

This zone is called the zone of intellectual capabilities because it controls the thought process, wisdom, and intellect of a person. The planets Mercury and Jupiter rule the memory zone, that's the reason this zone of the forehead is called the memory zone. This zone plays a vital role in shaping the destiny of a person as Jupiter is the ruler and the Guru of the demigods and all the planets. It is a self-illuminating planet and Mercury rules thoughts and perception. So, how wise a person is, and how strong or powerful a person's memory is, will be reflected by this zone. Now, let us individually discuss the effects of the Line of Mercury and the Line of Jupiter upon the destiny of a person.

a. Line of Mercury

Mercury is known as Buddha in Sanskrit. Please don't mistake this Buddha with Lord Buddha. Buddha here refers to the planet Mercury. Linga Purana states that Mercury is the son of the Moon by his wife Rohini. However, in *Vishnu Purana, Brahma Purana, Padma Purana, Vayu Purana etc.,* it is stated that Mercury was born after *Brahaspati's* (Jupiter) wife Tara was seduced by the Moon. Buddha, or Mercury, is called Saumya, i.e. son of Soma (Moon), so from him springs the lunar race. Even though the Moon (Mercury's father) is friendly towards Mercury, Mercury is always in conflict with the Moon, who seduced his mother, because he considers himself to be the son of Jupiter's wife.

Mercury is a neutral planet, and changes according to its place in a sign and house, and that's the reason it is said to have a 'mercurial' nature. Because it is nearest to the Sun it is restless, which makes it fickle. It changes quickly, and is often in retrograde. It sometimes precedes the Sun, and sometimes follows it. Mercury can be seen as a shining star in the morning and evening, and sometimes even during the day as well because of the power of its radiation. Being the Lord of Geminii, Mercury has two faces. Bile, wind, and mucus are the three doshas (faults) that dominate Mercury, so it is a shudra by caste. However, Mercury loves the company of learned people and is a merchant by nature. Its day is Wednesday; its colour is green; its gemstone is emerald; and it is the ruler of number five in Indian numerology.

In general, Mercury rules thinking and perception, processing, and disseminating information and all means of communication, commerce, education, and transportation. The presence of the Line of Mercury on the forehead indicates the conscious mind and the intellectual power of a person. People who have this line are generally accommodating, versatile, and dazzling. Symbolically, these people are mediators and the epitome of all good virtues and talents. Mercury's influence can give a person real originality, realisation, and genius. Mercury also symbolises language, speech, mental, and intellectual flexibility, education, mobility, and perception. It also represents a person's logic, skills, and expression in speech and writing. By extension, Mercury helps people who work in these areas, especially those who work with their mind, or wit, such as writers and orators, commentators, critics, doctors, teachers, travellers, scientists, etc. People with the Line of Mercury are therefore endowed with knowledge, and a flair for writing.

If the Mount of Mercury is not placed properly and has been tainted by the presence of moles or inauspicious marks, then Mercury makes the person sly, tricky, critical, deceptive, fraudulent, and quarrelsome. The person nags and gossips. There is no peace of mind, nor any inner substance and stability. Since Mercury can cause quick changes between extremes, it is associated with the element quicksilver. On a physical level, Mercury rules over the nerves and the brain. It is the centre of one's thoughts, memory, as well as speech. So the absence of the

Line of Mercury on a person's forehead will definitely take away these qualities and its ill placement can cause derangement, delusion, false wit, and difficulty in judgment and understanding.

b. Line of Jupiter

Jupiter in Sanskrit is known as *Brahaspati,* or *Guru.* Jupiter, is the Guru of demigods. It is a giant self-illuminating planet, and the centre of a mini-solar system of its own (Jupiter has over 60 known moons). A massive force, it radiates more energy than it receives, in keeping with its role as the Lord and the teacher of the demigods. This is a very auspicious planet and the presence of the Line of Jupiter on the forehead indicates 'Greater Fortune' (or 'Greater Benefice', Venus being the 'Lesser Benefice'). Jupiter governs joy, luck, and well-being.

The nature of Jupiter on the forehead relates to the expansion of horizons, or growth in higher understanding. The placement of the Line of Jupiter on a person's forehead helps define his higher level of thinking. Often, this placement gives clues about one's views related to weightier issues of life such as religion, philosophy, and social issues. Jupiter also rules optimism in living,

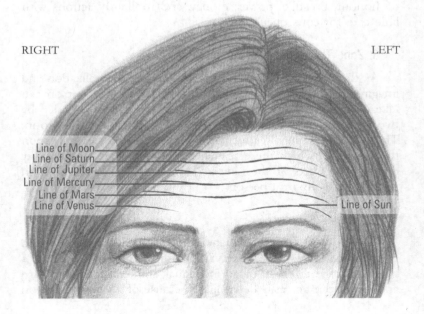

RIGHT   LEFT

Line of Moon
Line of Saturn
Line of Jupiter
Line of Mercury
Line of Mars
Line of Venus
Line of Sun

prosperity and growth, both mentally and physically. Jupiter governs one's interests in faraway places, travel, foreigners, academic, and higher education. Being a risk-taker, Jupiter also rules gambling, speculation, adventure, and moving into an unknown territory.

Jupiter is masculine, disciplined, co-operative and priestly. It rules our potential for growth and expansion on many levels such as physical, intellectual, spiritual, and cultural, while helping in the accumulation of material assets, power, and status. It is also exalted as a healer. Jupiter describes our optimism and aspirations, but also rules cultural pursuits, religion, highly structured positions of power, government, and matters of state. Everyone with high ambitions — priests, religious teachers, politicians, ministers, and people in the legal profession definitely possess the Line of Jupiter. Jupiter bestows peace, spirituality, and progeny. It also indicates a good relationship with progeny.

Jupiter's day is Thursday; its colour is yellow; its gemstone is yellow sapphire; and it rules the number three in Indian numerology.

The wrong placement of Jupiter leads to over-confidence, loss of honour, prestige, power, money, and foolhardy actions with little care for consequences.

3. Zone Three, the Imagination Zone

As the name itself suggests, this zone rules visualization and imagination. So how much flight the thoughts of a person can take is reflected by this zone. The imagination zone is ruled by two major planets in astrology, i.e. the Saturn and the Moon. These planets generally affect people differently, depending upon the houses in which these planets are present. Let's individually discuss the effects of the Line of Saturn and the Line of Moon upon the destiny of a person.

a. Line of Saturn

The Line of Saturn is situated just above the Line of Jupiter. Even if the lines in the observation and memory zones are not present on the forehead of an individual, still the Lines of Saturn and Moon can be easily determined because of their presence on the topmost part of the forehead. In astrology, Saturn is associated with restriction and limitation. Where Jupiter expands, Saturn constricts. In Sanskrit, Saturn is called *Shani,* or *Shanaishchara* (the slow mover), because it takes about two and half years to pass through each constellation of the sidereal zodiac. The *Markandeya Purana* states that Shani is the son of the Sun by his wife Chaya (shadow).

Saturn is a cold, dry, and lethargic planet. Saturn's sight is bad as it destroys the house it occupies, except if positioned in the seventh house, where it receives directional strength. A well-placed Saturn brings structure and meaning to our world. It also gives wisdom, spirituality, fame, integrity, patience, sincerity, authority, long life, leadership, and organisational abilities. It also endows awareness, strength, courage, self-control, and love for justice. An ill-placed Saturn brings miseries, sorrow, delay, obstruction, difficulties, defamation, and dejection. It also results in nervousness, depression, loneliness, inferiority complex, secretive, and defensive behaviour.

Generally, Saturn takes approximately 29½ years to complete its orbit around the Sun and to return to its birth position in the chart. So people with the influence of Saturn tend to be successful after the age of 30. People with Saturn's strong influence need to be excessively cautious in order to avoid penalties. Decisions made by these people around the age of 30 will determine their lifestyles and careers for the next 30 years. The same transformation can be seen around the age of 59-60, when these people will observe significant transitions and changes in their lifestyles and thought processes.

Highly structured positions of power, bureaucracies, and all forms of hierarchical systems are ruled by the Saturn, so people with an auspiciously placed Saturn, will become corporate giants, government officials, and great politicians. However, if Saturn's energy in the chart is exaggerated, it can result in tyranny and dictatorship. The image of Saturn is also that of a 'Great Malefic' because it can destroy your hard work, spoil plans, and delay success. So people with the Line of Saturn on their forehead should definitely get their faces read by a bona fide spiritual master.

Not only people with the Line of Saturn, but everyone who

needs an exact interpretation of his/her life, and who is honestly interested in finding a permanent solution for their miseries should work under the proper guidance of a bona fide spiritual master.

People with the Line of Saturn usually possess 'Saturnine' dispositions which are marked by lack of humour. These people are also authoritative, rigid, un-relaxed, and strict. A Saturnine disposition also demands that one follows strict rules and regulations, rituals, and strong moral values, only then will the individual become successful and get respect in society. People with the strong influence of Saturn, who have the discipline, will tend to rise high above the skies, however those who do not have the discipline, will certainly be vanquished by the blow of fate.

Saturn also represents ridicule for ineptitude, feelings of inferiority, and a sense of inadequacy. Such people need to work very hard to deserve anything throughout their lives. People influenced by Saturn's energy need to have deep maturity to attain success and to grow and expand. That's probably one of the reasons why these people most often attain success after the age of 30. As maturity is the significant element of Saturn's energy, so you can see a marked difference between the people who are not yet 30, and those who are over the age of 30, if they are ruled by Saturn. Saturn's day is Saturday; its colour is black; and blue sapphire is its gemstone. Saturn rules the number eight in Indian numerology.

b. Line of Moon

There is a Vedic verse which states *'chandrama manso jatah'* which means the Moon was born from the mind of the Supreme Personality of Godhead. Moon is called Chandrama in Sanskrit. Moon is the presiding deity of the element water and rules over the tides of the sea. The position of the Moon at the time of birth is very important because it will determine the internal constitution of a person. The Moon's sign, house, and phase can tell a lot about a person's emotional instincts and habits.

The Moon is auspicious for those who are born in the ascending Moon cycle and malefic for those who are born in the descending Moon cycle. The Moon controls emotions. It is the instinctual self. Moon reflects the power of the inner light, channelling, and moulding the shape of our personality. The Sun stands for character, and the Moon stands for nature. Our inner consciousness, instincts, sub-consciousness, private life, and the most intimate part of our self, are determined by the Moon's energy. People under the heavy influence of the Moon, or those who have the Line of Moon are extremely emotional, sensitive, dreamers, moody, and fickle-minded. The auspicious influence of the Moon bestows illumination, intuition, imagination, sensuality, sense of purpose, love for fine food, and arts. It also brings refined taste, values, money, wealth, power, wisdom, and good fortune. But, success is difficult for people whose Moon is not correctly placed. These people also become weak and sick, and it becomes difficult for them to live a comfortable life.

The Moon orbits the earth in 28 days, spending a fleeting 2.33 days in each sign of the zodiac. The Moon rules the fourth house, the house of home and family. The day of the Moon is Monday; its colour is white; its gemstone is pearl; its metal is silver; and it is the ruler of the number two in Indian numerology.

The Moon shows its influence when the person is around the age group of 24-25. This is the time when the creative abilities of the person possessing the auspicious Line of Moon flourishes. People with an auspicious Moon might become poets, artists, writers, singers, dancers, musicians, astronauts, scientists, inventors, discoverers, magicians, and numerous other things that are related to a powerful mind. These people's minds carry them to variegated lands, where it is generally impossible for any person with normal abilities to reach. These people generally think beyond the horizons of anyone else's capacity and create things that are absolutely astonishing and amazing.

Vedic physiognomy is of the opinion that an individual should neither have less than three horizontal lines upon the forehead; nor should he have more than three horizontal lines on the forehead. Three horizontal creases are considered to be the most auspicious in terms of reward and fulfilment. People with three horizontal lines upon their foreheads reach supreme positions in their lives, if other auspicious lines and marks on the face support them (like vertical lines on the forehead etc.) and if the face is auspiciously built. It should be noted that the forehead of Lord

Shiva has only three horizontal creases.

It is also stated that if an individual possess more than three horizontal lines upon his forehead then this is an indication of worry, inner strife, tension, anxiety, feelings of disturbance, desperation, and sometimes depression. So, in most cases, more than three lines on the forehead indicates conflicting situations within a person, which results in worry, fear, tension, anxiety, confusion, despondency, loss of memory, reason, will-power, etc. Finally, the person will experience failure in one's mission.

It is generally seen that people who possess more than three horizontal lines on their foreheads are extreme thinkers. These people tend to worry a lot. Their mental energies are divided in many directions and because of this they become confused. So they might succeed in nothing.

The Lines of the Sun and Venus should not be counted as two lines, because the Sun and the Venus rule only the halves of a particular zone. Again, it is worth noticing the combination of which three lines a person possesses, because the results will be according to those combinations. Less than three horizontal lines on the forehead, i.e. only two horizontal lines on the forehead is representative of a mediocre life. One line on the forehead represents a below than average life, and no line on the forehead is representative of a life full of difficulties, misery, and poverty. If a person possesses one or two lines on the foreheads, and if those lines are situated high above the forehead in the imagination zone, then these people will have to strive a lot in life and might have to start struggling at a very early age, or might have to struggle till late in their lives. Many lines in the imagination zone indicate that this person worries and frets a lot. Multiple lines on the forehead represent a lot of worry and anxiety.

Three horizontal creases along with the central axis and the third eye region are counted as the five mounts of the forehead. Horizontal mounts of the forehead control sensory perceptions while the central axis and the third eye region control a person's extra sensory perceptions.

CHAPTER 2
. . . .
VERTICAL LINES
ON THE FOREHEAD

1. Single Straight Line in the Third Eye Region

If there is a single vertical line in the third eye region, i.e. exactly in the middle of the eyebrows, then this gives a person unique powers and control over material affairs. A line in the third eye region indicates extraordinary powers and administrative skills. These people are highly influential. They possess the unique skill of influencing people and groups belonging to their levels. At whatever position these people might be, they will definitely have control over others who lie in their sphere of influence.

However, a vertical line in the third eye region does not indicate any kind of spiritual superiority. So, if a person has a vertical line in the middle of the eyebrows, it should not be assumed that a person is a great transcendentalist, or a master of Yoga and divine consciousness. Divine consciousness is always indicated by the central axis region. A vertical line in the third eye region is indicative of control and authority in material administration. People with a vertical line in the third eye region have lots of patience and stamina. They do not react very quickly. They have the tendency to control their anger for a very long period of time, which is ordinarily not possible for an average human being. These people do not express their anger very frequently, and without any purpose. As children, they will be very sweet and obedient, and will not go against their parents wishes very often. So as children, these people are tolerant, even if their parents are unjust. It is only when they grow up, that they start venting their anger sometimes. This is one of the most important reasons why these people are able to control others, because they themselves possess unparalleled control over themselves, and their emotions.

A vertical line in the third eye region is of two types — the suspended needle, and the deep cleft exactly in the middle of the eyebrows in the third eye region.

a. Suspended Needle

These are lines that seem like a suspended needle in the middle of the eyebrows in the third eye region. These lines indicate authority and control, but do not have the same kind of influential power as possessed by people with a deep cleft in their third eye region.

b. Deep Cleft in the Third Eye Region

These lines in the third eye region possess more depth and breadth than the previous category. These lines are not in the form of thin lines like that of a suspended needle, but are like a deep cleft (which is actually formed in the skull). If this person's forehead is X-rayed, we will find that there is a cleft in the skull exactly in the middle of the eyebrow in the third eye region, right since birth. This rift, or cleft, in the skull takes the form of a deep and shallow line in the third eye region, exactly in the middle of the eyebrows. This line is compared with the third eye of Lord Shiva by ancient transcendentalists and face readers. These people are born with unmatched power, devotion, authority, influence, and administrative skills. They possess the ability to sway the minds of people and to make devoted followers, who are ready to give and take lives if they receive just one gesture from these people. Unique administrative skills, combined with unflinching determination, unalloyed devotion, unparalleled patience, tolerance, and wisdom make these people a storehouse of power and authority.

Now, everything has different effects upon males and females, because of the way the brain and emotions function in both the sexes, so it should be kept in mind that the effect of a vertical line on the forehead is not similar for both sexes. As women are more emotionally functional, this feature (their emotional natures combined with a vertical line in the third eye region) brings rigidity and stubbornness in their characters. These women become strict, adamant, and hard from within. Becoming hard does not mean that a person has become more apt in controlling the emotions. It only means that the person has more suppressed emotions, which can come out at any point of time because those who control their emotions become softer and swarthier in their behaviour and actions. These women possess very domineering, rigid, and controlling natures. The marriages of these women get delayed very often, sometimes till an indefinite period.

2. Two Vertical Lines between the Brows

If there are two vertical lines starting near the heads of the brows then this represents a diplomatic person. People with these lines are also very suspicious and do not trust others easily. They are very cautious when it comes to any kind of dealings with others. If the other features on the face indicate a selfish nature, then some of these people might also be very selfish. Most of these people are very shrewd. Even if they are not shrewd, they project themselves to be shrewd, since these two

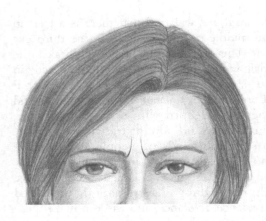

vertical lines between the eyebrows can only be created by the regular contraction of the eyebrows, and only those who are in doubt, suspicion, who wish to thoroughly scan things under their sight, will contract their eyebrows very often. Because of their uncertain and unpredictable nature, it is generally very difficult for others to understand them, so most of these people (especially women) will not have a long lasting relationship.

3. Three Vertical Lines between the Brows

There can be three vertical lines between the brows only when one line is present exactly in the middle of the brows in the third eye region, and the other two are near the heads of both the brows. As the vertical line in the third eye region signifies power and authority, and two vertical lines near the head of the brows signifies diplomacy etc., so these lines together will form an auspicious combination for the person concerned. These people won't be uncertain like the people in the previous category. These people will definitely be cautious and suspicious and will scrupulously formulate their judgements and opinions, however they won't always be doubtful and uncertain about everything because the line in the third eye region provides directional power as well. Most of these people are situated in the topmost positions of honour, authority, and power. This happens because they handle people and positions of power very diplomatically. It should however be noted that for women a vertical line in the third eye region is not very auspicious and delays their marriage, apart from creating conflicts in personal and business relationships. However, this word of caution is not for women who are very elevated souls and who work on the spiritual plane, or who possess divine consciousness. It should also be noted that three vertical lines in the brow region can also indicate a peevish, self-indulgent, and selfish character (especially in women).

4. Broken and Wavering Vertical Lines

If there are two vertical and wavering creases beginning at the head of the brows then this indicates unfortunate incidents in a person's life. It also indicates a life of severe tension and stress especially in the later years. These people might get affected by  misfortunes in their early twenties as well. This also indicates disastrous and criminal temperaments, particularly if three broken and wavering creases are present between the brows. These people tend to gain advantage of others using ruthless and dishonest means.

5. Crossed Vertical Lines

If the vertical lines in the brow region are crossed by horizontal lines, it represents conflicting situations within the individual. There is continuous strife and disturbance within these people, due to which they become indecisive and live in depression, sadness, and melancholy. These people also get

worried and irritated very soon due to continuous strife within themselves; most of them might end their lives due to p e r m a n e n t frustration.

6. More than Three Vertical Lines between the Brows

More than three vertical lines between the brows are not considered auspicious for the person who possesses them. Instead of many vertical lines, it's better to have no lines between the brows, because people with many vertical lines lack direction in life. These people are very fickle-

minded and restless and cannot concentrate upon a particular task.

7. Divine Chakra in the Central Axis

The central axis is significantly the most important position on the forehead and in the whole face, because this region represents the topmost chakra. Apart from being the storehouse of power, this region is also the region of divine consciousness. This region is represented by a Divine Chakra, or a wheel, which is very rarely found. This Divine Chakra is the rarest of rare marks or symbols on the forehead which is situated only on the foreheads of people who are divine incarnations. These divine incarnations might not

be the incarnations of God, but will definitely be the incarnations of elevated souls, who take birth on this planet from other heavenly planets. A person who visits ancient temples and museums in India will see this chakra depicted on the foreheads of Gods including the Supreme Personality of Godhead Sri Krishna. There are many statues of Vishnu, Narayana, Krishna, or their incarnations like Buddha that will have the Divine Chakra in the central region of the forehead. People who are really interested in Vedic face reading should definitely visit the museums and ancient temples in India and carry this book along with them, so that they can practically see and observe all the things mentioned in this book.

8. The Region of Virtue

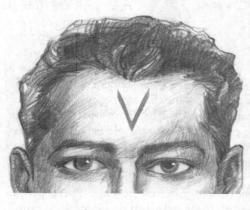

This region is situated in the central axis and is represented by a V-sign. It must be noted that the divine charka can be anywhere, above or below the V-mark, however in most people the V-mark is found holding or supporting the divine chakra (i.e. the divine chakra is placed above the V-mark). As soon as the person contracts his eyebrows the V-mark will immediately become visible. This mark bestows astounding intelligence to these people so that they may deal and tackle different situations and circumstances in this material world. These people possess unique wisdom, consciousness, concentration powers, and are equipped with material and spiritual knowledge.

People with the V-mark are also very enlightened beings. Their extra-sensory perceptions are very well developed. These people can sense future events much before its occurrence, with their highly developed extra-sensory perception. They also do not make any mistakes when they judge people, and situations. These people will also be very fair and unbiased in their decisions. They are also honest and loyal towards their subjects and do not waver from their mission easily.

9. Crown of the King/Trident

Sometimes the vertical grooves combine in such a way that they form a crown of the king on the brow, or the Trident on the fore-head. These symbols are very unique and rare and are found on the faces of very few people in the world, one in a billion. People on whose faces the crown of the king or the Trident is formed are blessed with power and good fortune. These people possess the power to sway masses and to bring happiness in the hearts of people just by their mere presence. These people generally possess a very expressive body language, and their power of expression is so strong that it acts like a stimulant and a magnet to stimulate and attract the hearts of many people, including friends, foes and strangers. These symbols denote a karmic reward. These people are careful observers and their wisdom is gained by their experience and by the combination of material and divine spiritual knowledge. These people might have faced certain disappointments in their early life, however final victory is inevitable after all the odds and oppositions. These symbols show that the individual's plans are in accordance with the divine plan and these people are helped and protected by demigods and angels. They also have the natural ability to charm others with their magnetic speech, refined wisdom, as well as with the grace and poise that they possess. Any person possessing the divine chakra, the crown of the king, or the Trident is not an ordinary human being. Great unconquerable emperors generally possess a combination of these marks. One of the predictions for these people is that they might leave such a mark on the pages of history, which will never be forgotten by the next generations.

CHAPTER 3

LINES AROUND
THE EYES

Lines around the eyes have a major significance in face reading. These lines explain the sexual behaviour of a person, as well as the behavioural pattern of an individual towards his/her parents and siblings. The upper and the lower portion of the eyes help in determining the exact behaviour of an individual with his parents and siblings.

1. Lines on the outer corners of the eyes

Crosshatched lines at the outer corners of the eyes represent an extremely sexual person. These lines are clearly evident when the person is smiling, or laughing. If these lines are seen on the faces of children, it should be understood that they are habituated to masturbation. These people also need many sexual partners when they grow up to achieve sexual gratification. Their sexual desire won't be quenched even after they become old.

2. Puffiness or Criss-Cross Lines below the Eyes

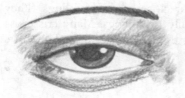

If there is puffiness, or crisscross lines, below the eyes, it represents an extremely heavy-hearted person. These people are dissatisfied with their parents, siblings, or spouses. Most of them might have been separated from their parents during their childhood. If there are many crisscross lines below the eyes then it represents the death of the father, or mother, or both at an early age. If these people are not given the proper environment for their growth and development, they might get involved in anti-social activities. Puffiness or criss-cross patterns below the eyes also represent that the past relationships of the person did not work properly, and the subject might have gotten separated from his/her beloved, or spouse, due to death, or divorce.

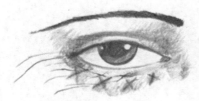

3. Criss-Cross lines above the eyes, between the Eyelids, and the Eyebrows

If a person has crisscross lines above the eyes, between the eyelids and the eyebrows, then he/she will have to leave home at an early age. These people are not close to their siblings. They might be estranged from their family, or siblings. Many crisscross lines in this region also represent that their siblings might have passed away at an early age.

CHAPTER 4

. . . .

FA LING LINES

Fa Ling lines are also called cheek lines, or laugh lines. These lines run from the nose, across the cheeks, towards the outer corners of the mouth. Fa Ling lines exist since birth, but are mostly visible when a person is smiling. These lines become more prominent on the face when the person crosses the age of forty. As the person approaches middle-age, these lines become clear and deep. These lines indicate the type of life a person will lead and the conditions he/she will experience. Fa Ling lines, or laugh lines, are very significant in face reading. An old proverb states, 'The one who laughs a lot, lives longer'. Fa Ling lines basically indicate how much authority a person will have through life, as well as the good, bad, and worst conditions a person might face in different periods of his/her life.

While reading these lines, it is very important to note the shape as well as the direction of these lines. In face reading, the person's life during his/her mid-fifties and early to late sixties can be determined by studying the Fa Ling lines. The specific age groups corresponding with these lines are 56, 57, 64, 65, 66, 67, 68, and 69. The shape and direction of Fa Ling lines will determine its impact on a person's life, specifically during the middle ages (after forty). However, it should be noted that the impact of Fa Ling lines are seen throughout one's life, right from birth till death. These lines are indicators of power and authority in the life of each and every individual.

Now, let us discuss the different types of Fa Ling lines and their impact upon an individual's life.

1. Broad Fa Ling Lines

Broad Fa Ling lines are broadly spaced away from the mouth. Fa Ling lines that run down the cheeks in a broad curve, away from the mouth are among the best categories when it comes to Fa Ling lines on the face. These people are capable administrators and are blessed with power and authority. They hold the topmost position in the fields of administration, government jobs, business, politics, as well as social and religious affairs.

People with broad Fa Ling lines are also blessed with creativity, so these people also prove their genius in creative and artistic fields like writing, acting, music, direction, filmmaking, fashion designing, photography, painting etc. These people will certainly establish themselves in their respective careers by the age of 30. Broad Fa Ling lines also indicate that these people will not have an unhappy mid-life, or old age, even if they might have had an unhappy childhood (because of being born in poor families, or because of some other circumstance).

2. Long Fa Ling Lines Running Down the Chin

Even if the Fa Ling lines are not broad, but if they run sharply down the face, without touching the corners of the mouth, and reach the chin, or the tip of the chin then these lines are also very good indicators of health and prosperity. These are also among the best Fa Ling lines. People with such lines live a long, healthy, and fulfilling life. These people will definitely live for more than ninety years, if other facial features do not indicate a fatal blow at an early age. They will not have problems related to finances as well, as there will be a continuous flow of money throughout their lives. Even if they are not born in rich families they will never fall short of money.

3. Fa Ling Lines Entering the Corners of the Mouth

Fa Ling lines that enter the corners of the mouth indicate bad luck, and ill-fortune. If these lines end after entering the mouth and do not continue lower down the chin, then these people will have a very rocky childhood and a very difficult life after the age of forty-five. These lines are also known as the 'starvation lines', because these lines indicate that no matter which position the person might achieve in his/her life, there will be a disastrous change during their mid-life, which will make them starve in some form (for love, money, friends, colleagues, etc.).

4. Fa Ling Lines Entering the Corners of the Mouth, or passing the Mouth at a Steep Angle and Continuing Down the Chin

If the Fa Ling lines do not end after entering the mouth and continue lower down the chin, or pass the mouth's corners at a

steep angle, and then run down the chin, then in both the cases the person concerned is his own worst enemy.

Firstly, these people are very blunt as well as rude and harsh, due to which most people turn against them. These people also get involved in useless arguments and unnecessary disputes. Secondly, they are extremely volatile and fragile. They do not keep their own word and promises, and hence they cannot be trusted. Thirdly, they have loose stomachs and might vomit out secrets anytime. Lastly, these people are extremely defensive and will never accept their faults easily and will always be adamant about their stance with complete disregard to the other person's viewpoints.

As Fa Ling lines entering the corners of the mouth are also known as the starvation lines, so there will be a disastrous change in these people's life as well, during their mid-life, which will make them starve for one thing or another. However, as these people possess another pair of lines that lead out of their mouths and continue downwards towards the chin, so they might encounter a disastrous turn in their lives, however they will be able to come out of it after a great struggle.

5. Locked Fa Ling Lines

If the Fa Ling lines join with the lip lines on the outer corners of the mouth then the Fa Ling lines are said to be locked. These Fa Ling lines are said to be locked because they do not proceed beyond the lock, which is set by the lip lines at the corners of the mouth. This type of Fa Ling lines are considered to be extremely unlucky as this makes the person accident-prone. The risk of accidents increases when these people enter mid-life. These people also suffer from poor health, indigestion, and stomach disorders.

If other facial features are strong then people with locked Fa Ling lines will not be disheartened, even if things go terribly wrong with them, as they never expect good things to happen in their life. These people will be able to turn misfortunes around most of the time and discover new directions after each and every downfall.

6. Locked Fa Ling Lines Breaking the Lock and Reaching the Chin

These Fa Ling lines are similar to the previous kind, the only difference is that when these Fa Ling lines are joined with the lip lines coming out of the corners of the mouth, they do not stop, and reach beyond the locks set by the lip lines and run down the chin. If these Fa Ling lines are deeply creased, then they are considered to be highly auspicious.

These Fa Ling lines suggest that these people will be able to establish themselves in the position of power and authority in spite of their enemies and detractors plotting against them. These people do not get easily scared or belittled even if someone is desperately trying to demoralise them. However, it should be noted if these lines enter the corners of the mouth, because if they do then they will possess the

features of starvation lines.

7.   Snake (Fa Ling) Lines

These Fa Ling lines are called Snake Lines because they curve twice or thrice. If the lines curve towards the mouth without touching the ends of the mouth and then again continue curving downwards towards the chin, then this suggests that the person concerned is accustomed to mood swings, is carefree and has a laidback attitude. These people always work as per their own whims and fancies and might often be completely reckless and careless.

8. Indistinct or Faint Fa Ling Lines

These Fa Ling lines are not very clear or distinct even when these people are laughing, or smiling. These Fa Ling lines are equivalent to non-existent Fa Ling lines. People with faint Fa Ling lines are not very lucky as they lack will-power. They do not have a strong will and fighting spirit, hence they are not able to reach higher positions of power and authority and are never able to advance much in their careers. They should take special care while making judgements.

9. Broken Fa Ling Lines

If the Fa Ling lines are broken and lack continuity then this represents an inauspicious destiny for the person. The owner of these Fa Ling lines will fall prey to the tricks and conspiracies of others and hence will face a lot of difficulties and might also get into trouble with the law because of this.

10. Unequal and Dislocated Fa Ling Lines

If the Fa Ling lines are unequal and dislocated, i.e. wander along different paths or directions from each other, then this is the indicator of an unstable and fickle-minded individual. These people lack persistence and hence they are not able to stick to their undertaken tasks. They also lack continuity. They might start a particular job with great enthu-siasm, however, they will easily leave it mid-way, either because of lack of interest, or because of lack of stamina.

These people are extremely faint-hearted and have lots of negativity within them. They might live a very poor life, especially during their old age and will face health hazards as well. These people face a galaxy of problems when they reach their fifties.

11. Upward-Turned Fa Ling Lines

If the Fa Ling lines are turned upwards then this is not considered to be an auspicious feature. People with upward turned Fa Ling lines do not possess good physical and mental health. The emotional quotient of these people might be too low and they might not be able to handle too much stress or pressure, because of which they might suffer from mental disorders and depression.

12. Double Fa Ling Lines

People who have double Fa Ling lines will have two Fa Ling lines on both the cheeks. One of the Fa Ling lines will start from the nose, run down from the sides of the mouth, and other will be on the sides of the cheeks, which will mostly appear when these people smile. People with double Fa Ling lines possess double the amount of power, authority and administration calibre as compared to those with single Fa Ling lines. These people achieve the topmost positions in the field of administration, government, business, politics as well as social and religious affairs.

People with double Fa Ling lines also possess very dynamic

mindsets. They are mentally very strong so they are rarely affected by the miseries of life. These qualities help them achieve success in any personal, or business, endeavour. Hence, they never face scarcity of money.

Most superstars, politicians, businessmen, and powerful people throughout the world possess double Fa Ling lines. People with double Fa Ling lines are extremely creative, so you will find most of these people in the fields of acting, writing, filmmaking, fashion designing, photography, music, direction, painting, and other artistic fields as they are multi-talented, versatile, and very dexterous.

13. Small Fa Ling Lines

Small Fa Ling lines start from the nose and stop before passing the mouth. These people possess poor health and might not live beyond the age of 55-60. They will also face lots of hardships in their lives and might lack money and resources to enjoy their lives to the fullest. However, it should be noted carefully if these people possess double Fa Ling lines, or broken Fa Ling lines. The second Fa Ling line will supersede the first and help out the smaller Fa Ling line neutralise the negative effects of the person's luck.

14. Mole on the Fa Ling Line

A mole anywhere on the Fa Ling lines states that the person concerned is always in strife with the world, and there is an inner strife going on within the person's head and heart as well. There might also be frequent twists in this person's life, and he/she might also be laughed at. A mole on the Fa Ling line also suggests

danger and a threat to the person's life when he/she is in the mid-fifties and sixties. This is because the Fa Ling lines are linked with one's mid-fifties and middle to late sixties.

American president Abraham Lincoln had a mole on his right cheek (on the Fa Ling line) and was shot dead at the age of 56. These people are also prone to accidents, so they should take every precaution and remain alert throughout their lives while doing something, or while going out of the house. One of their drawbacks is that these people are not able to maintain permanent careers and relationships and have the tendency to shift from one job, or relationship, to another.

PART IV

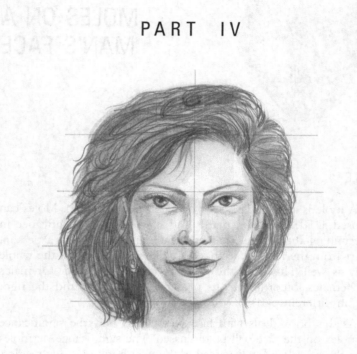

Moles

MOLES ON A MAN'S FACE

MOLE

A mole is a small dark spot or blemish on the skin. Moles can be used as identification marks and have a major significance in determining the nature, character, fate, and destiny of a person. Apart from the face, moles have a great significance on the whole body as well. However, the functions of moles differ for males and females, according to its presence on the left and the right side, in different parts of the face and the body.

As this book deals with face reading, so only the significance of moles on the face will be discussed. The significance of moles upon the body can be discussed in the next book on body reading.

MOLES ON A MAN'S FACE

Mole on the ears

Ears with moles are generally considered auspicious. Moles on the ears indicate unique intelligence and excellent wealth.

1. If the mole falls on the upper portion of the left ear it indicates that the person is extremely lucky. These people will have good luck in terms of higher studies and wealth. These people might not have been born in a very rich family; still they will have constant cash flow throughout their life.

MOLES ON A MAN'S FACE

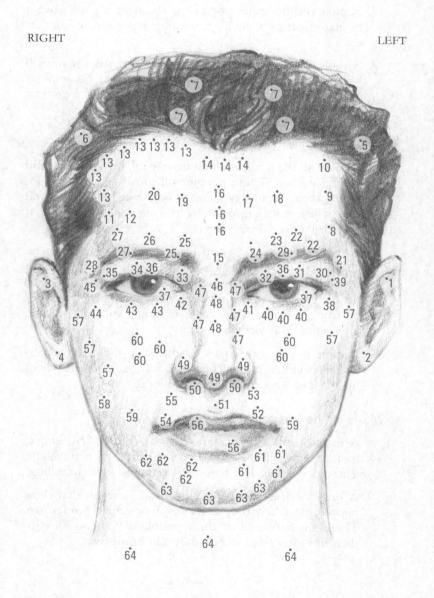

2. Mole on the earlobe of the left ear indicates high intelligence. These people might become writers, or may enter intellectual fields which will make them prosperous, and will improve their condition of living.

3. A mole on the upper portion of the right ear will have a similar effect as a mole on the upper portion of the left ear.

4. A mole on the right earlobe indicates that the person will have children who are very pious and reverent. Such moles are generally considered very lucky in terms of begetting wonderful offspring.

Mole on the scalp

5. A mole on the left scalp indicates a cool, loyal, honest, and careful person. These people will move and travel a lot during their life; however they should take precautions and care while travelling, as there is a fear of some kind of loss, or damage during travel.

6. A mole on the right scalp brings travel and movement. These people will travel a lot in their lives and will do a lot of research and development work, if the mole is located on the extreme right above the right ear. Their wives will be from a wealthy and fortunate family and will be wise, intellectual, and virtuous.

7. A mole on any other part of the scalp indicates success and recognition in life. Their wife will be from a family of high status, wise, intellectual, and loyal.

Moles on the forehead

8. A mole on the extreme left forehead (on the left temple) indicates one who is prone to accidents when travelling. These people need to be greatly cautious while travelling.

9. A mole on this part of the forehead indicates that these people die when they are away from their hometown. There are chances that these people will spend most of their life away from their family and hometown.

10. A mole on this part of the left forehead indicates fortune, talent, and big wealth. These people receive money easily through benediction and charity.

11. A mole on the extreme right forehead (on the right temple) indicates lots of wealth. These people might travel to distant lands and earn lots of money through their engagement in business and merchandise.

12. A mole on this portion of the right forehead indicates lots of wealth that might be inherited.

13. A mole on this part of the right forehead indicates bad luck to the parents, i.e. the mother, or father.

14. A mole exactly in the upper middle part (or somewhere near the upper middle part) of the forehead indicates fortune and longevity. These people live a stress-free life because all the monetary needs are taken care of by destiny and luck. There are good chances of travelling abroad. However, these people are quite rebellious (as children also) and they are their own bosses. They are better off taking care of a business, as entrepreneurs, and being self-employed, rather than working for someone else.

15. A mole in the third eye region is not considered to be auspicious. These people are foolish and possess explosive tempers. Generally, these people have very high opinions about themselves. They are also very argumentative, open, blunt, and impulsive.

16. A mole exactly on the central axis, above or below it, bestows the person with extremely good luck. These people are blessed with creative genius and managerial skills. They are generally original in their approach and are independent in their behaviour and lifestyle. It should be noted that if the mole is very big, or black, then it destroys all the fortune, luck and blessings, and brings misfortune instead.

17. A mole on the left side of the central axis indicates higher position, and huge success with the combined effects of wisdom, hard work, and destiny.

18. A mole on this position on the left side of the forehead is related with idea, integrity, and wealth.

19. A mole on the right side of the central axis indicates luck. This man is a man of action who is full of confidence and prefers to speak through his actions rather than his mouth.

20. A mole on this position on the right side of the forehead indicates a man of pride.

Meaning of moles above and within the eyebrows

21. A mole on the extreme corner of the left eyebrow will bring misfortune. These people might meet with accidents while travelling.

22. A mole on this position of the left eyebrow indicates wealth and luck in a person's life.

23. A mole above the middle of the left eyebrow indicates a position of power and authority.

24. A mole in the beginning (or above the beginning) of the left eyebrow indicates creativity and artistic skills.

25. A mole in the beginning (or above the beginning) of the right eyebrow bestows a person with wisdom, power, and supreme luck.

26. Mole above the middle of the right eyebrow indicates nobility, high thinking, poise and dignity.

27. A mole just before the corner of the right eyebrow indicates luck and fortune.

28. A mole on the extreme corner of the right eyebrow indicates labour throughout life. These people will have to struggle a lot, and work very hard to gain money.

Moles within the eyebrows

If there is a mole within the eyebrow and it is hidden, then it is considered to be a good omen in terms of fortune. A person with this kind of eyebrow will be good in dealing with finances. However, if the mole is large and prominent it represents quite an opposite case. People with large and prominent moles display their fortune ostentatiously, and tend to spend more than what is required. These people are also very extravagant and hence a large mole indicates a person's inability to save money, and others will try to usurp their finances.

29. Beware if a person has a mole exactly in the middle of the eyebrows or even slightly lower than that, or has big and visible moles. Spouses of people with such moles (in the middle of the eyebrows), and moles visible within the eyebrows, tend to die, or divorce after marriage. The chances are more for females with such moles rather than males.

Meaning of moles below the eyebrows

30. A mole below the corner of the left eyebrow indicates that the person is disaster prone and brings ill-fortune to himself, as well as to his spouse.

31. A mole below the middle of the left eyebrow means that this person brings ill-fortune to the spouse and is prone to accidents, especially in water.

32. A mole below the beginning of the left eyebrow indicates that the person is highly fortunate and will get a position of power and authority, especially in the government.

33. A mole below the beginning of the right eyebrow is a good indicator of wealth and prosperity.

34. A mole below the middle of the right eyebrow means that the person is disaster prone and prone to accidents with fire.

35. A mole just below the corner of the right eyebrow indicates misfortune and struggle throughout the life for survival.

Meaning of moles on the eyelids

36. Men with moles on the eyelids (on either side of the eyelids) are full of conflicting situations and contradictions within themselves. These men are not very intelligent, nor are they steady in their task. They are very self-centred. Their choice of friends and colleagues is also poor.

Moles inside and around the eyes

37. Moles on the cornea indicate impediments on the path of growth and development. These moles check material and spiritual progress. People with moles in their eyes have to suffer a lot in the hands of nature and other people. Moles on the cornea also indicate that these people will worry and fret a lot, especially about their children.

38. Moles anywhere near and below (not above) the corner of the left eye indicates extreme good luck in terms of money and fortune and an active sex life.

39. A mole anywhere above the corner of the left eye indicates misfortune.

40. Moles below the middle and anywhere around the middle of the lower portion of the left eye indicates lack of fertility, inability to reproduce, or chances of losing progeny.

41. A mole anywhere below the tip (beginning) of the left eye indicates misfortune and bad luck to parents, siblings, and progeny.

42. A mole anywhere below the tip (beginning) of the right eye indicates misfortune and bad luck to parents.

43. Moles below the middle and anywhere around the middle of the lower portion of the right eye indicate bad luck and suffering to parents, wife, or children.

44. A mole anywhere near and below (not above) the corner of the right eye indicates an uncontrollable sexual desire throughout life, even after aging.

45. A mole anywhere above the corner of the right eye indicates disaster.

Moles on the nose and on different places upon the bridge of the nose

Moles on the nose are considered to be extremely unlucky in every sense. Moles on the nose indicate that a person will have some obstruction to a healthy cash flow. There will also be an incident in these people's life between the ages 41-50 when they will lose a lot of money.

46. People with a mole in the beginning of the bridge of the nose are prone to losing their spouse, because of divorce, or death. This mole also results in infamy and character assassination of the person concerned.

47. Moles surrounding the bridge of the nose on the left and the right sides represent misfortune to one self and one's spouse. It also brings health hazards and a tendency to succumb to illness.

48. A mole exactly in the middle of the bridge of the nose results in lack of financial resources and strenuous monetary conditions. These people tend to waste their money upon futile things like gambling, sex, drinking, smoking, etc. They also might suffer from health hazards, or get caught by law which might result in draining their finances.

49. A mole on the tip of the nose indicates an overly sexual person, or problems related to sex.

50. A mole on the nostril (on either side of the nose) indicates that people take advantage of this person, or problems created by others due to this person's lust and greed. These people are highly sexed and very greedy, and might go to any extent to fulfil their greed and quench their lust.

Moles on the philtrum and the area above the upper lip

51. A mole on the philtrum generally indicates good health and longevity. This mole also indicates wonderful progeny. These people will be surrounded by friends, family, children, and grandchildren till the last moment of their lives. Their family and children will be very caring and supportive.

52. A mole on the left side of the upper lip indicates fame and recognition. These people will have plenty to eat and drink through their lives. Most of them generally have a satisfying home and family life.

53. A mole just below the left nose or anywhere near the nose is not fortunate and brings misfortune in some way or the other.

54. A mole on the right side of the upper lip brings fame and recognition, however conflicting situations also arise at the same time because of their habit of speaking uselessly. However, these people are happy-go-lucky as they will not face scarcity of food, or drinks, and will have a healthy and satisfying life.

55. A mole just below the right nose or anywhere near the nose shows health hazards etc. These people are very greedy and get trapped in problems created by others, or by people close to them, because of their greed.

Moles on the lips

56. A mole on the lips generally has different effects upon the person, according to the size of the mole. Generally, people with moles on their lips are very curious. These people also tend to speak a lot. Because of their talkative nature, they generally tend to make friends quickly. However, these people will not be able to keep secrets for a very long time, because they have loose stomachs (especially those who possess big moles). People who possess big moles on their lips are destined to get into trouble by speaking uselessly. People with moles on or around their lips are also highly sexed and enjoy eating a lot.

Moles on the cheeks and jaws

57. A mole exactly on the upper jaw hinge and the areas surrounding this place (both on the left and the right sides of the face) indicates longevity. Moles closer to the ears indicate excellent intelligence, and blessing to succumb and

rule people.

58. People with moles on the lower part of cheek (that are located far away from the mouth nearing the jaws) are capable of gaining lots of wealth, fame, and fortune at a very early stage of their adulthood, before reaching their thirties. These people are advised to tread cautiously, to maintain their wealth and status till their old age. Moles on both sides of the face on the lower jaws are not favourable, because although the person will get success and money at an early age, they might lose all their wealth, fame, and fortune because of being arrogant and big-headed about their success. For males, moles on the right side of the jaw are more favourable.

59. Moles on the lower part of cheeks (closer to the mouth) are not considered to be fortunate. These people are prone to accidents in water, or accidents due to their desire to seek thrills, or due to a fall. People with moles on the sides of the mouth do not have control over their mouths, and they tend to speak anything without considering the consequences. These people are prone to arguments and will only harm themselves because of this habit.

60. Moles in the middle of the cheeks are unfortunate.

If the combination of moles on the jaws and the cheeks make a triangle on the right side of the man's face then this man will be divinely blessed with wealth, beauty, power, wisdom, and fortune. However, it should be noted that moles on the cheeks should not be located in the middle portion of the cheek, and should be located in the areas of beard growth.

Moles below the lower lip and on the chin

61. A mole anywhere below the left side of the lower lip indicates high intelligence, luck, and fortune. These people will be very intelligent and will gain wealth and fortune as a legacy from somewhere. There are chances that these people will gain lots of wealth. These moles also indicate abundant sex.

62. A mole below the right side of the lower lip indicates abundant food, drink, and sex.

63. A mole anywhere on the chin (especially on the lower portion) represents a person driven by lust.

Moles on the neck and the throat

64. Moles anywhere on the neck (especially on the throat) indicate a lot of stress and pressure, both for men and women. Moles anywhere on the neck may also indicate a short life (death by accident, etc.), especially if the mole is located on the throat, or somewhere near the base of the neck. These people might also possess suicidal tendencies, because stress, pressure, tension, and anger are unbearable for them.

65. A mole or birthmark on the nape of the neck indicates a fault in the character. This mole indicates that the person will be harmed, or suffer an accident, it also indicates a short life. If this kind of mole is located on the base of the nape of the neck, then it indicates suicidal tendencies.

CHAPTER 2

MOLES ON A WOMAN'S FACE

MOLES ON A WOMAN'S FACE

Moles on the ears

Moles on a woman's ears are generally considered auspicious, like for men, however they have a slightly different interpretation.

1. If the mole falls on the upper portion of the left ear, it indicates unique intelligence. However these women are of the 'give me' type, i.e. these women believe in taking rather than giving.

2. A mole on the left earlobe indicates wonderful and pious children for these women.

3. A mole on the upper portion of the right ear will have somewhat the same meaning for women, as the mole on the upper portion of the left ear.

4. Moles on the right earlobe help these women get good husbands. Their husbands will be highly educated and wealthy.

Moles on the ears also indicate that this woman's first child will be a son. Women with long earlobes live a very long and healthy life. However, these women might be very adamant sometimes, because long earlobes indicate great will-power.

MOLES ON A WOMAN'S FACE

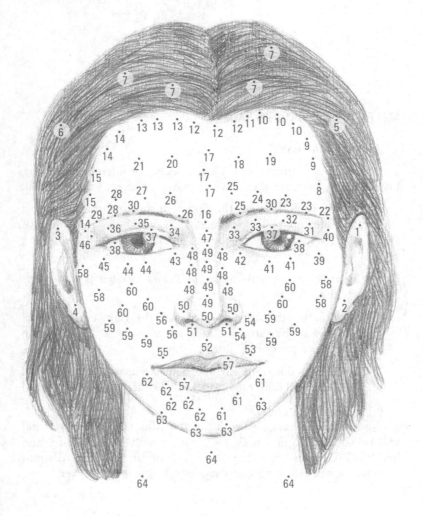

Moles on the scalp

5. A mole on the left side of the scalp indicates a neat, gentle, polite, generous, kind, and intelligent woman.

6. A mole on the right side of the scalp brings travel and movement for the women. However, she should take precautions and care during her travel as there is a fear of some kind of loss or damage during travel. She will also do a lot of research and development work during her travels.

7. A mole on any other part of the scalp indicates success and recognition in life.

Moles on the forehead

Moles on different parts of the forehead will have different meanings for women. The significance of moles on different parts of the forehead from the left to the right side of the forehead is as below.

8. A mole on the extreme left side of the forehead (on the left temple) indicates someone who is prone to accidents while travelling.

9. A mole on this part of the forehead (on the left temple) indicates the chances of some complications during delivery.

10. A mole on this part of the left forehead indicates extreme sexual lust.

11. A mole on this part of the forehead brings bad luck to the husband, and family.

12. A mole exactly in the upper middle part (or somewhere near the upper middle part) of the forehead indicates a rebellious and free-spirited women. These women will have many sexual encounters, or remarriages.

13. A mole on this part of the forehead indicates bad luck for parents, husband, and in-laws.

14. A mole on this part of the forehead indicates extreme sexual lust.

15. A mole on the extreme right forehead (on the right temple) indicates disaster for these women.

16. A mole in (or near) the third eye region (i.e. above or below) is not considered to be auspicious for women (as in the case of men). These women are foolish and possess explosive tempers. Generally, these women have very high opinions about themselves. They are also very argumentative, open, blunt, and impulsive. In most cases the marriages of these women will not last long, and divorce is inevitable. If the marriage lasts, it will end with the death of the husband.

17. Moles or birthmarks on (near) the central axis indicate that the women are generally independent in their behaviour and lifestyle. However, if the birthmark or scars in the third eye region, or central axis are ugly, or if there is a big mole in any of these regions, or if the mole is extremely black and ugly, then regardless of sex, the person will be doomed to ill-fortune.

18. A mole on the left side of the central axis indicates good luck.

19. A mole on this position of the left side of the forehead brings good luck in marriage, wealth, and fortune.

20. A mole on the right side of the central axis indicates luck.

21. A mole on this position of the right side of the forehead indicates women of great self-respect, ego, haughtiness, and pride.

Moles above and within the eyebrows

22. Women with a mole on the extreme corner of the left eyebrow will bring misfortune to themselves, their husband, as well as their families.

23. A mole on this position of the left eyebrow indicates good luck in marriage.

24. A mole above the middle of the left eyebrow indicates good luck, wisdom, and fortune.

25. A mole in the beginning (or above the beginning) of the left eyebrow indicates creativity, and artistic skills.

26. A mole in the beginning (or above the beginning) of the right eyebrow bestows a woman with creative genius, wisdom, fortune, and artistic skills.

27. A mole above the middle of the right eyebrow indicates a happy married life.

28. A mole just before the corner of the right eyebrow indicates respect, self-esteem, and pride.

29. A mole on the extreme corner of the right eyebrow indicates disaster, a tendency to be harmed, and extreme sexual lust.

Moles within the eyebrows

Hidden moles within the eyebrows are considered to be a good omen in terms of fortune for women. However, large and prominent moles indicate loss of money.

30. A mole within the middle (centre) of the eyebrows, or within the eyebrows that are visible means that the marriage will not last long for these women and death (of spouse), or divorce, is inevitable.

Meaning of moles below the eyebrows

31. A mole below the corner of the left eyebrow indicates that these women bring disaster to themselves, and ill-fortune to their spouses.

32. A mole below the middle of the left eyebrow indicates that these people bring ill-fortune to their spouses, and are prone to accidents especially due to water. These moles also suggest arguments.

33. A mole below the beginning of the left eyebrow shows that these women bring good luck to the husband and children.

34. A mole below the beginning of the right eyebrow is a good indicator of wealth and prosperity.

35. A mole below the middle of the right eyebrow indicates a secure and stable life for women in their relationship and career.

36. A mole just below the corner of the right eyebrow indicates misfortune, and a tendency to be harmed.

Moles on the eyelids

37. A woman with a mole or birthmark on the eyelid has very little respect for culture and tradition. This woman will always attract the company of bad men in some way or the other, and will never be content and happy in her family life.

Moles inside and around, or below the eyes

38. Eyes with moles on the cornea indicate impediments on the path of development and growth of a person.

39. A mole anywhere near and below (not above) the corner of the left eye indicates a voracious sexual appetite.

40. A mole anywhere above the corner of the left eye indicates misfortune and disaster.

41. A mole below the middle and anywhere around the middle of the lower portion of the left eye indicates lack of fertility, inability to reproduce, bad luck for the children, and constant worries about something, or the other.

42. A mole anywhere below the tip (beginning) of the left eye indicates misfortune.

43. A mole anywhere below the tip (beginning) of the right eye indicates misfortune due to accidents.

44. A mole below the middle or anywhere around the middle of the lower portion of the right eye indicates lack of fertility and misfortune.

45. A mole anywhere near and below (not above) the corner of the right eye indicates an uncontrollable sexual desire within these women throughout their lives, even after aging.

46. A mole anywhere above the corner of the right eye indicates disaster.

Moles on the nose and in different places upon the bridge of the nose

Moles on the nose are considered to be extremely unlucky in every sense, for women and men. There will also be an incident in these women's lives, between the ages 41-50, when they will lose a lot of money.

47. Women with moles on the beginning of the bridge of the nose are prone to accidents and strife.

48. Moles surrounding the bridge of the nose on the left and the right sides bring misfortune. It indicates accidents and health hazards and a tendency to succumb to illness.

49. A mole exactly in the middle of the bridge of the nose (or anywhere upon the bridge of the nose) indicates misfortune.

50. A mole on the tip of the nose indicates that the woman will have extreme sexual cravings (or problems related to sex). These women might get involved in many sexual escapades.

51. A mole on the nostril (on either side of the nose) indicates that the woman is fun-loving. These women are highly sexed and very greedy, and might go to any extent to fulfil their greed and quench their lust. These moles also indicate bad temper, problems created by others or advantage taken by others.

Moles on the philtrum and the area above the upper lip

52. A mole on the philtrum is generally an indicator of good health and longevity. These women will produce wonderful children.

53. A mole on the left side of the upper lip indicates fame, recognition, food, clothing, and sex.

54. A mole just below the left nose or anywhere near the nose is not fortunate and brings misfortune in some way or the other.

55. A mole on the right side of the upper lip brings fame and recognition. However, conflicting situations at the same time because of the word of mouth as these women involve themselves in lots of gossiping and have loose stomachs. However, this mole indicates cravings for fine food, drink, and sex.

56. A mole just below the right nose or anywhere near the nose, represents a galaxy of symptoms like health hazards, greed, accidents (especially related to water), low self-esteem etc.

Moles on the lips

57. Moles on the lips will have more or less the same impact upon men and women (refer to moles on a man's face).

It should be noted that women with moles anywhere on or around their lips are highly sexed and crave for nice food, clothes and money. Women with moles anywhere on or around the mouth are also habituated to fibbing and giving false promises and commitments (which they rarely intend to fulfil).

Moles on the cheeks and jaws

58. A mole exactly on the upper jaw hinge (both on the left and right sides of the face) and the areas surrounding this indicate longevity. Moles closer to the ears also indicate excellent intelligence.

59. Moles on the lower part of cheeks are not fortunate for women. Women with moles on their cheeks will create problems for themselves and will axe their own feet.

60. Moles in the middle of the cheeks are unfortunate.

Moles below the lower lip and on the chin

61. A mole below the left side of the lower lip indicates abundant food and drink.

62. A mole below the right side of the lower lip indicates high intelligence, luck, and fortune.

63. Moles anywhere on the chin (especially on the lower portion) indicate a highly sexed woman who enjoys and lusts after fame, wealth, recognition, and fortune.

Vedic physiognomy is of the opinion that people with mole/moles on the chin (both men and women) are not reliable and trustworthy. They might also have poor characters.

Meaning of moles on the neck and the throat

64. A mole anywhere on the neck or the throat of women will have the same meaning as for men (refer to moles on a man's face). However, Vedic face readers are of the opinion that the first child for these women is a boy.

65. A mole or birth mark on the nape of the neck has the same meaning for men and women (so refer to the explanation for moles on a man's face).

PART V

Analysis of Critical Features
through Face Reading

DIVINE AND DEMONIC NATURES

Divine and demonic natures can be easily interpreted in face reading either by looking at any single facial feature, or through the combination of different types of facial features. The Vedas state that, among all the people born on this earth, some are totally divine, who descend from higher planetary systems to enlighten the common masses; some are common people who are trapped in the clutches of *samsara* because they do not know the correct path to self-realisation; while others are totally demonic by birth, who arrive on this earth from different hellish planets. A person who is a master face reader can immediately understand whether a person has a divine consciousness, or demonic consciousness, at a single glance.

There are a few common features on the face that indicate the divine birth of a person.

STUDY OF DIVINE FEATURES

There are different features on the face and the body which are indicative of divine consciousness. If a person possesses very big and beautiful eyebrows and big eyes, trance eyes, or lotus eyes that sparkle then these are representatives of a higher consciousness. However, only the type of eyes and the eyebrows are not enough for determining the exact consciousness of a person. The divine consciousness of a person is also determined by the marks on the forehead and from the type of ears a person has. For example, if a person has large ears and earlobes like that of Lord Buddha, then the person is said to have divine consciousness, however the other parts of the face should not be ignored. The back part of the head is also very important in calculating the intelligence and consciousness of a person. A protruding back head indicates a high intelligence quotient and can become a divine feature if coupled with other divine facial features. However, it should be noted that if a person does not have other auspicious and divine features then a protruding back head alone does not have much value.

In face reading, the most powerful divine features are located on the forehead. The divine consciousness of a person can be determined by looking at the forehead alone. There are four signs on the forehead that are representatives of divine consciousness. The first sign is the divine chakra near the central axis. The second is the V-mark near, or above, the central axis. The third is the deep cleft in the skull in the third eye region which is the mark of the divine presence of the third eye. And the fourth is the crown of the king, which is the combination of different creases on the forehead. If the person has three of the aforementioned four signs upon his forehead then he will definitely be considered to be a person of divine birth.

It should also be noted that the cleft in the third eye region does provide a person with unique influential abilities, but if a person only has a cleft and does not have the divine chakra, or the V-mark then the person might not have divine consciousness. For example, one of the demons named Shishupala was born with the third eye, however he possessed demonic qualities and was therefore killed by the Supreme Personality of Godhead. If we look closely at the deities in Vedic literature, we find the presence of the divine chakra and the V-mark on the forehead of Lord Vishnu and the third eye on the forehead of Lord Shiva. Lord Shiva is also portrayed with three horizontal creases upon his forehead, apart from the third eye, which represents patience, resolve, and firm consciousness. For a fledgling face reader, it might be very difficult to initially identify the features which are representatives of divine consciousness; however, one can achieve perfect knowledge about mystical sciences by association with learned *acharyas* and from transcendentalists who represent the disciplic succession of spiritual masters. This is so because while learning spiritual sciences it is very important that one learns them in the most correct and bona fide way. It is also very important that one should not get confused by different marks and signs on the faces and bodies of different deities, because only those features are highlighted in the paintings and statues of the deities which describes them most appropriately, as it is not possible to include all the features of the deity in a single statue, or painting. So as far as mystical teaching of Vedic face reading is concerned, one should learn and understand it through the most authentic source.

Again, it should also be noted that several features of the body also play an important role in determining the exact constitution of a person, so one should not ignore the body. That's the reason why it is always suggested that one should get a reading done from a bona fide spiritual master, who is thorough in all the subjects, and not from a neophyte, who is just in the process of learning face reading, body reading, or other Vedic sciences.

One of the most important tasks in face reading is how to read a criminal's profile and to establish the potential features of criminals, so I will discuss that briefly in this section. There are various facial characteristics that indicate demonic qualities, which can be seen in different parts of the face. Let's discuss all these traits.

STUDY OF CRIMINAL PROFILES (DEMONIC NATURES)

1. Protruding Forehead with Receding Hairline

Protruding foreheads with receding hairlines make a lethal combination. The person might most probably be a deadly and a dangerous criminal, especially if the subject is female. It should be noted that individually also (without the combination of receding hairline), a protruding forehead is typical of great criminals. In protruding foreheads, either the front part of the head will stick out in an exaggerated manner, or the mounts of Venus and Sun (which are both above the eyebrows) stick out. In both conditions, a person becomes very lethargic, sensual, wanton, lewd, dissolute, and dumb. As these people are very hot-blooded, so they lose their hair (in most cases, if not all) at a very early age in their life. It should be noted that one of the reasons for losing hair is high sex drive. One of the reasons why over-sexed people lose hair very early is because their head remains hot most of the time, due to excessive sexual heat.

It should however be noted that not all people with receding hairlines are criminals. Receding hairlines at an early age definitely has a link with sex and pleasure, however for a person to become a criminal, some of the planets in his zodiac must be misaligned. And protruding foreheads represent the inauspicious situation of some of the planets, according to the part of the forehead that protrudes. So a protruding forehead definitely represents demonic nature, and if these protruding foreheads are supplemented with baldness at an early age then this indicates that the person is working in the mode of ignorance with full demonic principles.

2. Multiple Lines on the Mount of Venus, or the Mount of Sun

Generally, only one line on the Mount of Venus or the Mount of Sun is favourable for a person. More than one line on the Mount of Venus, or the Mount of Sun explains an exaggeration of desires within a person. These people are generally maniacs when it comes to material things like sex, power, or pleasure. If the person possesses two lines of Venus or Sun then also the drive for pleasure and power is more, but the appetite is controlled, if one is motivated enough. However, if a person has three or more lines of the Sun or Venus, then the appetite for pleasure and power is beyond the control of a person. It is not that people with three or more lines of the Venus or Sun cannot control their urges, but it is very difficult for them to control these urges until and unless they are trained in a spiritual way in different processes of yoga and spirituality. It is generally seen that serial rapists and killers generally possess more than two lines of Venus on their foreheads, and great tyrants possess more than two lines of Sun on their forehead.

3. Recessed Back Heads

When it comes to recessed back heads, the back of the head is not developed fully. The rear part is either recessed or flat, which means that the rear part of the head is not as developed as it should be. People with a recessed back part of the head generally have low levels of understanding. They also possess a revengeful nature and most of them are prone to high-blood pressure and anger. These people overreact very easily and tend to get violent within moments. People with recessed back heads generally fall into the demonic category because of their nature.

4. Protruding Brow Bones

It is generally seen that people who possess demonic natures, have over developed lines of Venus and Sun, or their mounts of Venus and Sun protrude. So protruding brow bones represent overtly developed mounts of Venus and Sun. As discussed earlier, when the mounts of Venus and Sun protrude in an unnecessary fashion this leads to lewd behaviour, tyranny, and extreme desire for sex, pleasure, money, or power. So people with protruding brow bones can be very dangerous and can turn deadly if this combines with other aggressive features on the face. Most of these people could be in the most wanted criminal list of the state, especially if the brow bones are protruding, as well as high.

5. Conspicuously Short or Fading Brows

Generally, short and fading eyebrows are indicators of demonic principles. As the eyebrows are located in the celestial region which belongs to the mode of goodness, so auspiciously built eyebrows play an important role in the formation of character and destiny of a person. Eyebrows govern desire, activity, and self-control. People with conspicuously short or fading eyebrows are filled with desire, however they lack direction in life. So the activities that these people perform revolve only around their desires. People with short and fading eyebrows also lack longevity. This happens mostly because most of them do not love their own selves. They generally possess a hedonistic approach towards life. They have a strong desire to have material things, more than morality and other virtues. Most of these people might be very high profile and hardcore criminals because they lack judgement and direction.

6. Eyebrows Joined in the Middle

Eyebrows joined in the middle have different impacts upon different people, depending upon the sex and other facial features. A negative impact is seen both in males and females, however the negative impact is more when the subject is female, rather than male. Females with eyebrows joined in the middle are wicked and cheats. These eyebrows are also a sign of divorce, widowhood, or lack of compatibility with the beloved. So, these women might get divorced, separated, or widowed in extreme cases. For men, these eyebrows represent a deep lust for women. In most cases, the man remains under the influence of women with negative traits, because of his lust for women. It should be noted that even if this eyebrow is considered to bring negativity in a woman's behaviour, attitude as well as life, then also these women should not be branded as criminals, without their other facial features being judged properly, as this feature alone is not sufficient to determine a criminal.

7. Arched Eyebrows

Like joined eyebrows, arched eyebrows should be studied carefully, if these eyebrows are coupled with other demonic traits. Arched eyebrows are one of the basic traits of criminals, if they are combined with other aggressive and criminal features on the face. It should be noted that if the arched eyebrows start fading by the mid-section then this could be one of the major indicators of a highly cruel and tyrant personality.

8. Brows Curved Upwards in the Beginning

Brows that are curved upwards in the beginning are not considered to be very auspicious for the person who possesses them. These brows are possessed by people who are cruel and fanatics. These people generally have a quick temper, and low tolerance levels. If other facial features indicate demonic traits then this person might be a professional criminal.

9. Round and Small Eyes Resembling a Fish

People with round eyes which resemble a fish are highly dangerous and could be suspects in criminal cases. It is generally observed that round eyes that resemble a fish are also widely open in most cases and such eyes are also traits of criminals and tyrants.

10. Widely Open Eyes

If the eyes of a person are open in such a manner that it seems as if one is applying a lot of strain upon the eyes then the eyes belong to the demonic category of widely open eyes. Hitler's eyes were like this.

11. Wolf Eyes

Wolf eyes are another category of demonic eyes. These people are very dangerous, deadly and harmful, so there is a possibility of their being criminals, and anti-social elements.

12. Puffy Eyes

If the eyes are always puffy then it represents some kind of continuous internal disturbance within the person. These people are highly disturbed and these eyes represent some kind of deep psychological imbalance. It should be noted that under these eyes there might be permanent bags, or permanent puffiness below the eyes.

13. Permanent Red Veins Visible on the Ears

People with permanent red veins on the ears possess cruel and fanatic dispositions. As these people have the tendency to be cruel, so there is every chance for these people to fall into criminal categories.

14. Tortoise Nose

As discussed in the chapter on the nose, people with a tortoise nose are mean, wicked and harmful and fall into the demonic category. Lust and insecurity draws these people towards criminal activities.

15. Cleft on the Tip of the Nose

Cleft on the nose represents the base, mean, and roguish nature of a person. As already discussed in the nose section, these people are the most selfish and are concerned only with fulfilling their own desires without thinking about morality. Vertical clefts are most commonly seen on the tip of the nose and horizontal clefts are seen on the sides of the tip. These people might not be on the most wanted list of the state, but are still very wicked and are concerned only with the fulfilment of their own ends. These people are mostly pretenders, but don't fall into the trap of their pretensions as they are highly demonic. This nose type is considered to be the worst type of nose in terms of character and integrity, so don't ever trust their words, or take them for granted. These people crave and hanker for money, sex and enjoyment throughout their lives.

16. Crooked/Deformed or Indented Philtrums

People with crooked, deformed or indented philtrums most commonly resort to crimes for satisfying their lusty nature.

17. Mouth Profile (Lips) Angled Downwards

In face reading, mouth profiles that are angled downwards are not considered to be very lucky because such lips, or mouths, fill a person with pessimistic and negative thinking. As these people are negative thinkers, so negative emotions and actions overtake their positive outlook of life. Most of these people are drawn towards criminal activities due to their despondency, frustration, deep anger, hatred etc. So, while reading criminal profiles this characteristic of the face should not be neglected.

18. Pursed Lips

Among all the demonic features in the face, pursed lips are one of the important facial features that represent a personality full of wicked and harmful intent. These people could be very deadly when it comes to taking revenge, or harming someone. Tightly clenched lips are representative of base, mean, roguish, and extremely harmful people.

19. Black Tongue

A black tongue indicates a demonic and wicked nature. However, while judging criminal profiles, this feature alone won't be sufficient in determining the criminal nature of a person.

20. Uneven Teeth

Uneven teeth represent faulty natures and wicked dispositions, so these people might get involved in criminal activities, if not always, then occasionally.

21. Spaced Teeth

People with teeth spaced away from each other are demonic in their temperament. These people do not have kindness within them, so if a person has spaced teeth and a few other negative features, then he/she is supposed to be guilty of the crimes he/she has been caught for.

22. Wide Cheekbones, or Cheekbones Closer to the Ears

Most of the criminals possess wide cheekbones, or cheekbones closer to the ears. This happens because wide cheekbones or cheekbones closer to the ears are representative of a highly aggressive personality and dominant nature. It is very difficult for these people to adjust to the laws of the state, or with society as they disregard any kind of authority, or restriction. If wide cheekbones or cheekbones closer to the ears are combined with wide jaws, then these people are definitely demonic and criminal in their nature.

23. Wide Jaws

As already mentioned, wide jaws could be one of the facial features which could determine a criminal profile, especially if the jaw width is greater than the forehead width and when the face generally has a slight upward triangular look. In this kind of triangular look, the lower part of the face looks broad because of the width of the jaws and the upper part of the face looks narrow because the jaw's width is greater than the forehead's width. As already discussed in the section on jaws, for these people the mode of ignorance is broader and the mode of goodness is narrower, so these people react quickly without second thoughts.

24. Extremely Broad Chin

People with extremely broad chins are tyrants, because they possess zero tolerance for others. This happens more if the chins are long, as well as broad, or when it is very long and jutting out, or broad and jutting out etc. So these people could be criminals if other features on the face also indicate such behavioural patterns.

While reading criminal profiles, it should be noted that many times, only a single feature of the face does not indicate whether a person is a criminal or not. A face is like a package, so the whole package should be considered before reaching any conclusion. For example, a criminal might not contain all the above mentioned features on his face, however he can still be a criminal because of the deadly combination of other features like the angular position of the nose, hooked nose, deformed nose, short and stocky ears, certain kinds of philtrums, bony or protruding jaws etc. The above mentioned features on the face have been listed because people with any of the above mentioned traits are more likely to be criminals than those who do not have the above mentioned features. However, reading criminal profiles is a vast subject and it will take a complete book to discuss thoroughly the details of different compositions of facial features. As this book is written keeping in mind the needs of the common people, so the information given herein concerns the common people.

IDENTIFICATION OF DIFFERENT DISEASES THROUGH FACE READING

Different diseases can be easily identified by looking at a person's face, if the face reader has a thorough knowledge of Ayurveda. The science of Ayurveda describes that the body is composed of five essential elements, which are Earth, Water, Fire, Air, and Sky. The interactions of these five elements produce three *doshas* (defects) within a person according to the combination of elements one falls into. These three *doshas* are:

1. *Vata Dosha*: Ether (Sky) and Air combine to form *Vata Dosha*. *Vata* is the force that directs nerve impulses, circulation of blood, respiration, and elimination.

2. *Pitta Dosha*: *Pitta Dosha* is formed by the combination of Fire and Earth. This *dosha* is responsible for all metabolic activity in the body.

3. *Kapha Dosha*: Ether (Sky) and Water combine to form *Kapha Dosha*, which is responsible for growth etc.

Of all the three, *Vata*, or wind, occupies a prominent position.

The balance of the body is lost and people acquire diseases if there is excessive agitation of any of these three *doshas* in relation to others. This loss of balance may be due to the result of excessive or deficient use, or misuse, of (1) the senses; (2) individual action (of body, mind or speech); or (3) acceleration of time, i.e. due to different seasons.

Deha-prakritis (Bodily-constitution)

The *tridoshas* result in the classification of different types of bodily constitutions which are known as *deha-prakritis*. The predominance of a particular *dosha* decides the constitution of an individual. Excess *Vata* (Air) results in *Vatiya* constitution. Predominance of *pitta* gives rise to *pittiya* constitution and a predominance of *Kapha* results in *shleshmaja* constitution. The body constitution is something that one is born with and there is no change till one dies.

Different bodily constitutions (*deha-prakriti*) have different dietary habits and peculiar responses to drugs. It should also be noted that as per the rules of Ayurveda, any medicine cannot be prescribed for the patient unless the constitution of the patient is known by the physician. This is so because a medicine which helps a particular type of bodily constitution won't help someone with a different constitution.

History and branches of Ayurveda

The main body of Ayurveda is found in the *Atharvaveda*. Apart from containing the description of various diseases (both physical and mental), the *Atharvaveda* also contains the cause of those diseases as well as the rules of correct diet and behaviour. It is said that Brahma imparted the knowledge to Daksha Prajapati, from whom it was passed on to Ashwinikumaras and from them to Indra (the emperor of Heaven). Lord Indra sent Lord Dhanwantari to this earth to impart the knowledge to others. Dhanwantari's student, Sushruta then wrote a famous treatise on surgery called the *Sushruta Samhita*. And finally, Charak wrote the famous treatise on general medicine, the *Charak Samhita*.

Ayurveda has eight distinct branches:

(1) General medicine

(2) Major and minor diseases

(3) Midwifery and paediatrics

(4) Aphrodisiacs

(5) Major surgery

(6) Psychiatry

(7) Toxicology

(8) Rejuvenation

Because of this eight-fold development, Ayurveda is sometimes also called the Ashtanga Ayurveda.

Among all the five elements Vayu (Air) is the originator of every kind of action in the body. It is called the *Tantra-Yantra Dhara* i.e. the maintainer of the human body, keeping it in shape. Vayu occupies pride of place among the three *doshas*. Just as the wind controls the direction of the clouds, likewise Vayu controls the functioning of *Pitta* and *Kapha*. Vayu is of five kinds: *prana, udana, vyana, samana*, and *apana*.

Prana Vayu is responsible for breathing, swallowing of food and the functioning of the heart. Food is moved into the stomach and blood is circulated in all parts of the body by the power of *prana vayu*, as all the parts of the body are directly connected with it. The *udana vayu* helps in maintaining the strength of the body by giving strength to the mind, intellect and memory. The *udana vayu* therefore becomes responsible for the production of action, speech, and various sounds within the body. The *vyana vayu* helps in secretion and perspiration and controls closing and opening of glands in the body. It also carries food juices, and controls the various movements of the body. The *samana vyau* is located in the navel region and is responsible for the actions of digestive enzymes. It helps in the digestion of food and transforms it into blood, semen, and urine. It also helps separate the vital nutrients from the waste products, and sends the waste to the large intestines. The *apana vayu* is situated in the region of the anus and the lower regions of the digestive tract and reproductive organs. It acts downward to expel the faeces, urine, semen, and foetuses.

As Ayurveda is a vast subject and this book is related to face reading, so only a synopsis of how to identify diseases through face reading is stated in this chapter.

Identification of diseases through face reading

To identify different diseases through face reading, one should be thorough with the specific facial areas that rule the inner organs of the body. These are as follows:

(1) The topmost part of the skull is ruled by the kidney

(2) The forehead signifies the bladder

(3) The area above the eyebrows is ruled by the gall bladder

(4) The area between the brows is ruled by the liver and the stomach

(5) The thyroid, liver, and kidneys are represented by the eyebrows

(6) The under eye region represents the stomach, kidney, and liver

(7) The cheeks and the nose represent the heart region

(8) The lower part of the cheeks and the jaws represent the lungs, stomach, and colon

(9) The side parts of the nose represent the lungs

(10) The ears represent the kidney

(11) The philtrum represents the spleen region

(12)   The portion above the upper lip represents the liver

(13) The stomach represents the upper lip

(14) The intestine represents the lower lip

(15) The areas below the ends of the mouth are represented by the colon

(16) The chin is ruled by the kidney and the bladder

SPECIFIC FACIAL AREAS THAT RULE THE INNER ORGANS OF THE BODY (ILLUSTRATION)

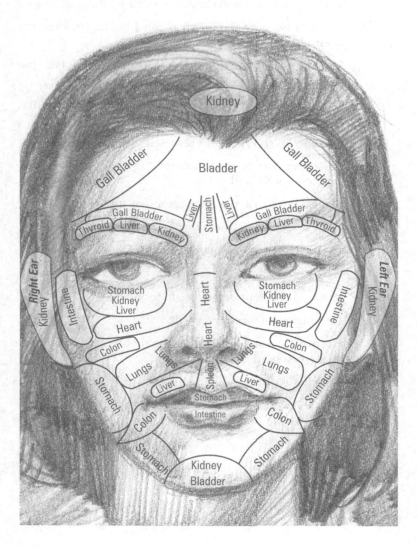

RIGHT   LEFT

As one needs to be thorough in the knowledge given in Ayurveda to understand the details of problems, or diseases, so just to avoid any confusion for a layman who is wishing to learn face reading, this section deals with simple methods to determine diseases. So, we won't be going into an in-depth study and analysis of this subject in this book, however one can definitely learn a few basic tips of how to determine the constitution of a person through face reading. Now let's analyse the constitution of a person through face reading.

1. Vertical lines above the ends of the eyebrows: As this position of the forehead is ruled by the gall bladder, so vertical lines in this region or anywhere else on the forehead indicates some complications, or stress in the gall-bladder. Spots and cross-hatched lines on the forehead also indicate congestion of the kidney and the gall-bladder. This can happen because of junk, oily, and greasy food, or excess of cigarettes and alcohol. A lot of stress upon the liver and gall-bladder can lead to dizziness, headaches, etc.

2. Cross-hatched lines in between the brows: Such lines indicate serious complications in a person's liver or stomach. In most cases these people are addicted to alcohol because of continuous inner strife and imbalance which might also result in liver damage.

3. Inauspicious marks just above the brows: This can result in high blood pressure, complications in liver, dizziness etc.

4. Fading brows: Eyebrows that start fading from the middle indicate thyroid problems.

5. Blue veins appearing on the cornea: If the cornea becomes blue in colour or blue veins appear on the cornea then this indicates some kind of problem in the liver, or kidney. It also represents depleting adrenal energy.

6. Yellow veins on the cornea: Yellow veins indicate some kind of complication in the liver, or kidneys. Permanent blue or yellow veins on the cornea might suggest that the liver or the kidney of a person might have been permanently damaged.

7. Puffiness, darkness or cross-hatched lines below the eye region: This feature indicates a lot of inner strife and disturbance within a person. Most of these people are addicted to drugs, alcohol, or other intoxicants. If there is puffiness as well as cross-hatched lines then this might indicate complications in the stomach, liver, or kidney. In some cases it indicates liver damage, especially if moles or other inauspicious marks are present in this region. Puffiness and darkening below the eyes also state depletion of adrenals due to improper sleep, worrying, drinking, or eating junk food.

8. Lines running down the cheeks from the corner of the eyes indicate some kind of problem in the kidney, or the intestine.

9. Redness of the ears: Redness of the ears states that the liver or kidney is stressed due to junk food, drinks, or tobacco. Redness of the ears also implies the depletion of adrenal energy.

10. Redness, puffiness, criss-cross lines or dark patches on the nose or around the nose represents some kind of problem, or congestion in the heart, or the lungs. This might happen due to excessive smoking, drinking, and use of oils or fatty food such as ghee (clarified butter). Mucus and congestion in the lungs can happen due to an improper diet.

11. The lips and the mouth represent the stomach and the intestines, while the part above the upper lip represents the liver. The stomach is also represented by the lower part of the face and the jaws. If the person suffers from constipation, or other stomach related disorders then boils and pimples appear on the lips and other parts of the face. Disorder in diet, excess in dairy, sugar, and junk food can cause soreness in the mouth, cracked lips, and pimples, or white spots in the lower portion of the face. White spots and blotchy areas might also point towards yeast infection. If the lips are dry, cracked, or rough then this indicates acidity and inner heat within the stomach. A protruding lower lip indicates a sluggish colon. Dryness around the

mouth indicates a lot of heat within the stomach and problems related to digestion or constipation.

12. Identification of diseases by studying the tongue:

i. If the tongue is red, blood red or unusually red, this indicates some serious health issues. These people either suffer from some major health problem, or nutritional deficiencies. A red tongue is basically a sign of different nutritional deficiencies.

If bright red patches are seen on the tongue which may or may not burn, this indicates hormonal changes. These patches are also caused by allergic reactions, or stress. These patches are harmless and usually go away by themselves, however sometimes anti-inflammatory medicines are prescribed for these conditions.

ii. Taste problems: Taste problems are generally caused by side effects of certain medications. This might also be caused by some kind of infection related to the tongue. However, it should also be noted that as the tongue is related to the neuro-membranes, so if there are persistent problems of taste, then that might also indicate nerve damage.

iii. Tremors in the tongue: Tremors in the tongue are basically caused due to neurological disorders and also due to an overactive thyroid gland.

iv. Difficulty in moving the tongue: If there is difficulty in moving the tongue, then this is definitely a sign of nerve damage.

v. Curling of the tongue: Curling of the tongue is caused due to a reaction to certain medication.

vi. Swollen and smooth tongue: The tongue becomes swollen because of some infectious disease, or sometimes due to very serious diseases. The cause of smoothness of the tongue is basically due to deficiency of vitamins, or anaemia.

vii. Painful tongue: There could be numerous causes for a painful tongue, such as cancer of the tongue, or the mouth, anaemia, oral herpes, etc.

13. Boils, pimples, redness, swelling etc. on the cheeks represent that the heart is not pumping enough pure blood. It also represents bowel problems, or constipation.

14. Boils, pimples, redness, swelling etc. on the chin represents problems in the kidney, bladder, stomach, or intestine. There may be some kind of congestion, weakness, or malfunction in these organs.

This is a brief synopsis of how to identify different health problems and diseases through face reading, however as already mentioned, going into detail is beyond the scope of this book as it will require a detailed explanation of the vast subject of Ayurveda.

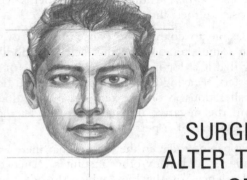

CHAPTER 3

EXAMINING WHETHER SURGERIES HELP ALTER THE DESTINY OF A PERSON

DO SURGERIES HELP ALTER THE DESTINY OF A PERSON, OR PURIFY THE CONSCIOUSNESS OF A PERSON AND NULLIFY THE NEGATIVE IMPACTS OF CERTAIN FACIAL TRAITS?

Lots of people throughout the world, especially in the West believe that surgeries that alter the face and the body can help level the negative impacts of certain facial or bodily features and can help bring peace, joy, and harmony to the individual, which is not true. People with such beliefs are in a disturbed condition of life and remain perturbed and disturbed even after undergoing multiple surgeries. Lots of so called pseudo-gurus who have opened shops related to different oriental practices, who do not have any bona fide spiritual background, leak out such information that if a person has some negative traits which are reflected by certain features of the face or the body, then that negative trait and its impact can be nullified by surgeries.

This is absolutely untrue, absurd, and rubbish. These pseudo-gurus promote such kinds of nonsense because they themselves are not aware about the corrective measures to nullify the negative impacts of negative features. They themselves are in a diseased condition of life and are patients of destiny. They actually think that since they are living a purposeless life, there is no reason why others should be happy, so they try and spoil the mission and purpose of another person's life as well. So these pseudo-gurus actually suffer from a *schadenfreude* syndrome as they themselves are waste matter, likewise are their thoughts.

It is not at all possible to change the consciousness of a person just by making some alterations in the facial and bodily features. It's like saying that if a dog is made to wear the hide of a lion then the dog will start behaving like a lion, which is false. So, just by making some alterations in one's exterior, a person does not become free from the negative impacts of one's karma, neither does the consciousness of a person change.

The thing that is happening today in the West is that there are many face reading institutes and many other institutes related to different metaphysical sciences of the East, which do not have any authentic background. The so-called show bottle institutes themselves do not have the perfect knowledge about anything but they still start teaching others and offer advice based on their impractical and imperfect knowledge. It is due to the result of such teachings, people's lives have been doomed to hell. The only way to purify one's consciousness and nullify one's past deeds is through the practice of very simple regulative measures as is stated in the Vedas.

However, to purify one's consciousness, one should first of all know what a human being is. A human being is not just the flesh and bones that we see, because flesh and bones alone cannot do the thinking without higher consciousness. So, to change the functions of those flesh and bones, we will first have to change the consciousness. But one should be aware how to bring about changes in the consciousness, only then can one bring about changes in the functioning of the entire body and only then will one be able to alter one's destiny. And to change the consciousness, one should be aware what the Vedas are about and what the functions of the Vedas is and to become aware about all this, a person has to first meet a bona fide Guru, who knows the real purpose and essence of the Vedas and the ancient mystical teachings of the Vedic literature. Unless one is able to do this, all his/ her attempts will go in vain and won't produce any results, neither will one be able to solve any purpose and eventually the purpose and mission of one's life will be spoilt.

Vedic literature is like the ocean of knowledge which has the cure for even the worst symptoms a living entity has. So a person who is thorough in the Vedic knowledge becomes a perfect entity on this earth to have the answer to every question and a solution for everything.

It is just common sense that one cannot change one's thoughts, actions, consciousness, and destiny by making some alterations in one's exterior, but still the western philosophers, face readers and pseudo-transcendentalists promote that a person can change his entire destiny by undergoing few modifications in one's face or the body. However, this is completely incorrect and it only reveals the meagre knowledge and gross stupidity of those philosophers as well as their followers. If somebody would have been able to change one's way of thinking, one's behaviours, actions, and consciousness by making some alterations in ones exterior then the masks of all the great thinkers, scientists, leaders, politicians, businessmen and all the corporate giants and billionaires would have been made and people would have had taken up their role just by using those masks. It's like saying that one can grow apples by sowing rice grains in a piece of land. It should be learnt and understood that breeds cannot be changed just by manipulating the exterior. A dog cannot possess the strength, aggressiveness and hunting abilities of a lion by wearing the hide of a lion. So no matter how hard these pseudo-transcendentalists and face readers might try to promote their wrong concepts, they will just end up giving the world the proof about how illiterate and unqualified they are in the field of spirituality and how their so called pseudo-metaphysical shops are cheating the common people of the world.

So instead of getting involved in useless gymnastics, a person who is really serious about this human life should search for a bona fide spiritual master who is in disciplic succession of Sri Krishna, to make a permanent solution for this material phantasmagoria. A bona fide spiritual master in disciplic succession of Sri Krishna is compulsory because Sri Krishna is the source of all the knowledge and of everything that is manifest or will manifest in the future. One who understands this is actually in knowledge and half of his/her job is done. The other half will be done once he/she is able to meet a bona fide Guru, expert in the science of Krishna.

VEDIC RESEARCH INSTITUTE

Hope you enjoyed reading our book. We welcome you to the Vedic Research Institute. We would like you to participate in our Vedic research program to help you enrich your experience. Vedic research institute welcomes and values your comments, suggestions and feedback as its aim is to provide you the most dynamic literatures of the Vedas which have been lost in haze of legends, with the momentum of time. We endeavour in reviving the ancient Vedic literature for the benefit of mankind. Please post your comments, suggestions and feedback so that we could enlighten you in a better way in the coming years.

Name: _____

Contact Nos: _____

E-mail: _____

Age: _____

Occupation: _____

Address: _____

_____

_____

City: _____ Pin Code: _____

Country: _____

How did you like this book?

_____

_____

_____

_____

_____

What changes did you see within yourself after the first reading?

_____

_____

_____

_____

_____

What expectations do you have from the Vedic Research Institute in the near future?

_____
_____
_____
_____
_____

Which Vedic texts/ facets/ forms of knowledge would you like the Vedic Research Institute to revive for you for your further betterment?

_____
_____
_____
_____
_____

Please let us know if you would like to be an active participant of the Vedic Research Institute and if you wish to elevate yourself to the Kingdom of God by donating/contributing for our speedy functioning and expansion: _____
_____

Queries: _____
_____
_____
_____

Your Views/Suggestions: _____
_____
_____
_____

Comments: _____
_____
_____
_____

Feedback: _____
_____
_____

SEND YOUR ENTRIES TO:
www.hrishikeshdubey.com or write to us at
contact@hrishikeshdubey.com.